————The QPB Companion to————

The Lord of the Rings

Quality Paperback Book Club
New York

Acknowledgment of permission to reprint previously copyrighted material can be found on page 103.

The QPB Companion to The Lord of the Rings is a publication of Quality Paperback Book Club, 1271 Avenue of the Americas, New York, NY 10020.

Edited by Brandon Geist

Cover image © The Tolkien Trust, courtesy Houghton Mifflin Company

Book design by Irene Lipton

Printed in the United States of America

CONTENTS

THE "DEPLORABLE CULTUS"

THE READER

Preface

E ver since I arrived at Cambridge as a student in 1964 and
encountered a tribe of full-grown women wearing puffed
sleeves, clutching teddies and babbling excitedly about the
doings of hobbits, it has been my nightmare that Tolkien
would turn out to be the most influential writer of the twentieth century," Germaine Greer wrote in 1996. "The bad
dream has materialized." Poor Germaine Greer. What must
she think to find that even the end of Tolkien's century did
not mark the end of Tolkien-mania? Instead it marked yet a
new beginning—a "return of the king," we might call it.

Tolkien is the king. Like his writing or not, one has to
marvel at the staying power of his epic trilogy, its magical
ability to draw new generations into its thrall. The story told
in the trilogy has fascinated readers for almost half a century,
but the story that can be told about the trilogy—the story of
its unlikely best-selling author, its contentious critical reception, its inestimable cultural influence—is fascinating in its
own right. The goal of this QPB Companion is to give you a
sense of that fascinating story; the larger goal is to encourage
you as a reader to become a part of both stories.

In the first section, "The Author," we meet J.R.R. Tolkien
himself—hardly the hotshot best-selling author of modern
day who is not only a writer but a pin-up, a performance
artist, and a pundit. Tolkien was instead a man that *The New
York Times* described as "the tweediest and most persnickety

of Oxford philologists;" a man who said of himself, "I am in fact a *Hobbit* (in all but size)"; a man who would not get his major work into print until he was sixty-two. An annotator and translator of Old English, Old Norse, and Welsh poetry, Tolkien created Middle-earth from the words up—building original languages derived from his studies and only afterwards realizing the need for characters to speak them. How did this English academic's thousand-page fantasy, born of a linguistic experiment, end up selling hundreds of millions of copies and consistently named in public opinion polls as one of the most beloved and influential literary works of the past century?

Despite its overwhelming popular success, *The Lord of the Rings* has hardly been universally acclaimed. In the second section, "The Critics," we look at the continuing debate over the literary merit of *The Lord of the Rings*. No one can dispute the trilogy's influence—the books practically created the genre of modern fantasy—but since its publication in 1954–55, *The Lord of the Rings* has met with a volatile mix of critical acclaim and derision. Chris Mooney's article "Kicking the Hobbit" provides a humorous survey of *Lord of the Rings* lit crit, and then we're headlong into highlights. In the immediate wake of the books' publication, Tolkien's good friend C. S. Lewis proclaimed the work an instant classic, while Edmund Wilson groaned, "Oo, Those Awful Orcs!" and called the trilogy nothing more than "juvenile trash." Years later, Ursula K. Le Guin and Isaac Asimov recounted their numerous readings and rereadings of *The Lord of the Rings*; Le Guin ranking Tolkien with Dickens and Tolstoy and confessing that the trilogy still makes her teary-eyed. Most recently, cultural curmudgeon Harold Bloom shed tears of another sort as he called the books "inflated, over-written, tendentious, and moralistic to the extreme." Even so, Bloom has, in a separate article, conceded that Tolkien's classic is, at the very least, better than the Harry Potter books . . . or rather, that the Harry Potter books are worse.

Next we turn to a group even more opinionated than the critics—the fans ... or as Tolkien himself referred to them—"The 'Deplorable Cultus.'" In this section, commentators look back on the "cultus" of yesteryear and look ahead to the promise of renewed Tolkien-mania. Surely the fanaticism that *The Lord of the Rings* spawned is one of the strangest, most impressive aspects of its literary saga. In the '60s, as the trilogy developed its cult following, one Berkeley bookstore owner commented that Tolkien-mania was "more than a campus craze; it's like a drug dream." If *The Lord of the Rings* was a drug, then the side-effects have been numerous and long-lasting—there are the slogans, from "Go, go Gandalf" to "Frodo Is God," in graffiti, on bumper stickers, T-shirts, or simply shouted; there is the Tolkien Society, the Mythopoeic Society, the Rivendell Group, Taruithorn International; and there is the dense swamp of fan artwork, poetry, and scholarship, most of it doubtlessly "deplorable" but some of it inspired. Certainly it is easy to see all this as pure silliness, but perhaps more than anything, it is evidence of just how beloved the books are and how much so many people wish to become themselves a part of the fantasy—here is a literary epic with the following of a rock band.

Finally, we invite you, "The Reader," to partake in the fun. There are reading group discussion questions sure to inspire some deep perusal and hearty debate, puzzles to test your Middle-earthly knowledge, recipes sure to make your stomach as rotund as that of a Hobbit, and maps to guide you through Tolkien's meticulous world.

More than most books, *The Lord of the Rings* has proven to be a wonderfully interactive experience, inspiring its readers to controversy, research, obsession, and creation; carving out a legacy that goes well beyond its own pages. You don't have to be an active fan bearing a Gandalf tattoo, writing odes to Hobbits, and regularly attending Tolkien conventions in order to be part of this legacy. And you don't need to be a disdainful critic railing joylessly against the moralism and adolescence of Tolkien's trilogy. All you have to do is read, read *The Lord of the Rings*, read the Tolkien miscellany assembled here, and you will be a part of the story, in your own way responsible for a very simple fact—Frodo lives!

—*Brandon Geist*

Introduction

THE LORD OF THE RINGS BY J.R.R. TOLKIEN: PERSONAL BEST

by Scott Rosenberg

Is it possible to love and champion *The Lord of the Rings* in 1996? Since it first swept college campuses in the 1960s, J.R.R. Tolkien's trilogy has spawned so many fourth-rate knock-offs, inspired so much bad fan art, and been so soundly and hilariously parodied that one hesitates to name it in serious company.

And yet, in an age when bogus myths of self-fulfillment like *The Celestine Prophecy* are peddled as best-selling truths, Tolkien's act of myth-creation retains a unique integrity. The Oxford scholar invented a rich world from the words up. A student of medieval tongues and legends, Tolkien began imagining his Middle-earth by creating a language, and then realized he'd need to dream up characters to speak it and stories in which it might be used. These stories "grew in the telling," as Tolkien put it, until finally they became Middle-earth's raison d'être, relegating Elvish and the rest of Tolkien's invented languages to footnotes and appendices.

Its linguistic roots still give Middle Earth a sense of internal consistency that also extends to its geography. Tolkien's marvelous maps are rich in some details yet suggestively fuzzy around the edges, hinting at mysterious landscapes on the borders of comprehension. As the avalanche of posthumous Tolkieniana that's been published over the last two decades has demonstrated, this writer approached his imaginary creations with the obsessive perfectionism others typically reserve for stories of their families or accounts of their psychological travails.

Still, *The Lord of the Rings* would never have found an audience of millions if it were merely a collection of a made-up world's maps, glossaries and chronologies. With his tale of an omnipotent ring and a diminutive hobbit whose lot is to destroy this cursed heirloom, Tolkien created a free fantasia on Norse and Celtic myth transmuted by the touch of two World Wars' horrors.

Reams of paper have been expended, and mostly wasted, on attempts to prove that *Lord of the Rings* is in fact an allegory of the Second World War or a Christian tract. But the books, passing the test of modern mythmaking, resist any one-to-one correspondence: their humane variation on the theme of good vs. evil cannot be reduced to a single lesson.

They are surely not perfect. The Cockneyisms that accompany Tolkien's portraits of his hobbits can grow tiresome, and the books contain little humor, pitifully few female characters and even less in the way of romance with a small "r." But as a vast vision of the absolute corruption of absolute power—and the depths of courage that ordinary people (and other creatures) can find to oppose it—Tolkien's work remains incomparable.

It's no coincidence that *The Lord of the Rings* first found its audience during a decade when the general public was learning to question the workings of power, globally and in their own lives. The trilogy's popularity stemmed not from the craven escapism critics found in its pages but rather from its opposite—a recognition that Middle Earth, in broad moral terms rather than crude allegorical parallels, is simply our earth, refracted in a fantastic mirror.

Today, who would dream of pasting a "Frodo Lives" sticker on his bumper? Yet the bookstores are more crowded than ever with people on "quests" to bring a sense of the "mythic" to their everyday lives. They could do far worse—and alas, too often they *are* doing far worse—than to take Tolkien's journey of a thousand pages.

—*Salon,* 2001

The Author

The Prevalence of Hobbits

by Philip Norman

H obbits adore tobacco and fireworks. So does Professor Tolkien, who first wrote "hobbit" thirty years ago on a dull exam paper he was correcting. At Headington, near Oxford United soccer ground, Tolkien has a study in his garage. Dark-topped tobacco tins are left like markers along his shelves; and there is a good view of the rockets if some college beanfest explodes them. "I run to the window," Tolkien confesses, "every time I hear a woosh."

John Ronald Reuel Tolkien was once kidnapped in South Africa and was, until 1959, Merton Professor of English Language and Literature at Oxford University. He has a square, big face, and his coat and cardigan, both gray, are rumpled slightly; he talks rapidly, with his pipe stem getting in the way. As well as hobbits—benevolent, furry-footed people, fond of bright colors—Tolkien has put into his books a grizzly man who can change into a bear, a thieving, English-speaking dragon, dark horsemen in the sky who cast freezing shadows, and a dreadful war in which thousands of goblins perish. He has spilled them into a separate world called Middle-earth and dressed them with names, lineages and languages which he explains in a 104-page appendix. The explanation is sending Americans, especially students, half mad with delight. One student's mother said, "To go to college without Tolkien is like going without sneakers."

There is a Tolkien Society of America and a *Tolkien Journal*. At a meeting of the society it is usual to lie around eating fresh mushrooms, a favorite hobbit food, drinking cider and talking about family trees, which no hobbit can resist. One must remember to call wolves *wargs*, goblins *orcs*, treelike people *ents* and the sun She. A popular greeting is, "May the hair on your toes never grow less." Everyone wears a badge with a slogan naming a Tolkien character: Frodo the hobbit or Gandalf the wizard; and louder enthusiasts chalk them on walls, sometimes in three-foot-high letters, preferably at the 116th Street-Columbia University subway stop. Tolkien books sell in student cafeterias next to the cigarettes; they have been translated into nine languages including Japanese and Hebrew and are part of the degree course at Liège University. Their world sales are almost three million copies, but it is the Americans who are wildest about them. An unauthorized paperback edition sold well over a quarter of a million copies. In the fifties, *World Science Fiction* called Tolkien the best fantasy-writer of the year and gave him a model rocket. "It's upstairs somewhere," Tolkien thinks. "It has fins. Quite different from what was required, as it turned out."

Tolkien is famous for two works: *The Hobbit*, which he began on that dull exam paper in the thirties, and his three-book saga, *The Lord of the Rings*, which Tolkien typed two-fingered. It ran to over 1,200 pages and took him fourteen years. *The Hobbit* told of Bilbo Baggins, who was press-ganged out of the Shire (the gentle, agreeable hobbit country) and into a venture to steal back treasure from a dragon, who was sleeping on it. But *The Lord of the Rings* was infinitely more grown up. In it, Bilbo's heir, Frodo, joined another expedition to break the grip of the Dark Lord of Mordor. This could be accomplished only by taking his ring, accidentally picked up by Bilbo, and destroying it in the gloomy and dangerous land where it was forged, under the very eye of the Dark Lord. The terrors on the way included a giant spider; goblins were savaged and savaged each other. The hobbits had to learn responsibility and resolution, and they were trailed by a horrid rubbery thing called Gollum (who placed eighth in an Ugly Man contest at the University of California at Berkeley).

The hobbits' long quest, wrote Edwin Muir in the *Observer*, "is a heroic conception. Tolkien's imagination rises to it though his style now and then fails him"—a remark calculated to plant in innumerable minds a little of the savagery of Shelob, Tolkien's giant spider. Tolkien's style, an amalgam of Celtic bard and Fowler's *Modern English Usage*, never ebbs. His people go deeper and deeper into situations from which paths stretch out of sight into ancestries and legends. Yet often they speak as if only mildly perplexed. In the midst of awful privation in *The Hobbit*, Gandalf the wizard says, "This won't do." Besides, an author who can create and sustain and make us revere a race of people resembling trees could never be failed by his style. These are the *ents*, the oldest people in the world. Sometimes they resemble a conclave of professors, and the most brilliant touch of all is that they have a sense of humor to match their age and knowledge.

Tolkien says, "My stories seem to germinate like a snowflake around a piece of dust," but he is tired by his work on the sequel to *The Lord of the Rings*, an even more somber story of a much earlier Middle-earth called *The Silmarillion*, in which there are no hobbits. People are constantly writing to Tolkien's publishers, George Allen and Unwin in London and Houghton Mifflin in Boston (often in the Elvish language Tolkien devised), to ask about the delay.

"Exhausting! God help us, yes. Most of the time I'm fighting against the natural inertia of the lazy human being. The same old university don who warned me about being useful around the house once said, 'It's not only interruptions, my boy; it's the fear of interruptions.'" (His wife, Edith Mary, isn't in good health, and Tolkien does a lot of housework.)

Tolkien has a three-bedroom, rectory-looking house in the Oxford suburb of Headington, with a back garden fence he built himself. Cars parking near the soccer ground force him to keep the garage gates locked. The study in the garage is filled with books and the smell of distinguished dust. It also contains a new tin clock and a very, very old, buff-colored portmanteau. "Portmanteau?" (It is scarcely visible under some newspapers.) "Oh, that. It was given to me by my guardian, who was half Spaniard. It isn't there for anything at all except that inside it are all the things I've been going to answer for so many years, I've forgotten what they are." Tacked onto Tolkien's window ledge is a map of Middle-earth showing the routes of the two hobbit expeditions, and a list of Tolkien's engagements, written in blue-black ink. A powder horn hangs over the door.

Tolkien wasn't a hearty child. At the age of three he was brought home from Bloemfontein, South Africa, his birthplace, and brought up at Sarehole, near Birmingham. Until he won a scholarship to grammar school, his mother taught him. He is particularly attached to the powder horn; it reminds him of being "borrowed" by an African named Isaac, who wanted to show off a white baby in his kraal. "It was typical native psychology, but it upset everybody very much, of course. I know he called his son Isaac after himself, Mister Tolkien after my father, and Victor—ha! ha!—after Queen Victoria.

"I was nearly bitten by a snake and I was stung by a tarantula, I believe. In my garden. All I can remember is a very hot day, long dead grass, and running. I don't even remember screaming. I remember being rather horrified at seeing the Archdeacon eat mealies [Indian corn] in the proper fashion." ... Tolkien stuck his fingers in his mouth.

"Quite by accident, I have a very vivid child's view, which was the result of being taken away from one country and put in another hemisphere—the place where I belonged but which was totally novel and strange. After the barren, arid heat, a Christmas tree. But no, it was not an unhappy childhood. It was full of tragedies but it didn't tot up to an unhappy childhood."

Sarehole has long since been eaten by buildings, but it was rather beautiful then. Tolkien was a shy little boy but friendly with the village children, and he knew an old lady without teeth who ran a candy stall. He modeled his hobbits on the Sarehole people, which means they must have been gentle amblers, not really fond of adventures but very fond of their food. Tolkien himself likes plain meals and beer; "none of that cuisine mystique." Beer, cheese, butter and pastry; the occasional glass of Burgundy.

"Hobbits," Tolkien says, "have what you might call universal morals. I should say they are examples of natural philosophy and natural religion." They are certainly capable of extraordinary bravery and humaneness: living in burrows, their creator declares, doesn't amount to anything like an animal kink.

"People still love thatched houses; they pretend it's because they're cool in summer and warm in winter, and they'll even pay a bit of extra insurance. We found German trenches which were often very habitable indeed except that, when we reached them, they faced the wrong way about. And have you been to England's oldest pub, the Trip to Jerusalem? It is carved out of the solid rock of Nottingham Castle. I went to Nottingham once for a conference. I fear we went to the Trip to Jerusalem and let the conference get on with itself."

Hobbits aren't small; nor are any of Tolkien's people. He says warmly, "I don't like small creatures. Hobbits are three to four feet in height. You can see people walking around like that. If there was anything I detested it was all that Drayton stuff; hideous. All that hiding in cowslips. Shakespeare took it up because it was fashionable, but it didn't invite his imagination at all. He produced some nice, funny names like Cobweb, Peaseblossom and so on; and some poetic stuff about Titania, but he never takes the slightest notice of her. She makes love to a donkey."

The Hobbit wasn't written for children, and it certainly wasn't done just for the amusement of Tolkien's three sons and one daughter, as is generally reported. "That's all sob stuff. No, of course, I didn't. If you're a youngish man and you don't want to be made fun of, you say you're writing for children. At any rate, children are your immediate audience and you write or tell them stories, for which they are mildly grateful: long rambling stories at bedtime.

"*The Hobbit* was written in what I should now regard as bad style, as if one were talking to children. There's nothing my children loathed more. They taught me a lesson. Anything that in any way marked out *The Hobbit* as for children instead of just for people, they disliked—instinctively. I did too, now that I think about it. All this 'I won't tell you any more, you think about it' stuff. Oh no, they loathe it, it's awful.

"Children aren't a class. They are merely human beings— at different stages of maturity. All of them have a human intelligence which even at its lowest is a pretty wonderful thing, and the entire world in front of them. It remains to be seen if they rise above that." Tolkien has a grandson who is becoming a demon chess player. The sound of children skylarking in the road doesn't disturb him, but he dislikes it when they fight or hurt themselves.

Tolkien says his mother gave him his love of philology and romance; and his first stories were gathering in his mind when he was an undergraduate at Exeter College, Oxford. When war came, however, he didn't write in the trenches as some chroniclers insist. "That's all spoof. You might scribble something on the back of an envelope and shove it in your back pocket, but that's all. You couldn't write. This [his study] would be an enormous dugout. You'd be crouching down among flies and filth."

His close friend, the late C. S. Lewis ("a very busy official and teacher" to whom Tolkien test-read a great deal) wrote once that the darker side of *The Lord of the Rings* was very much like the First World War. He gave examples: the sinister quiet of a battlefront when everything is prepared; the quick and vivid friendships of the hobbit journeys and the unexpected delight when they find a cache of tobacco. No, Tolkien says, there is no parallel between the hundreds of thousands of goblins in their beaked helmets and the gray masses of Germans in their spiked ones. Goblins die in their thousands. This, he agrees, makes them seem like an enemy in a war of trenches, "But as I say somewhere, even the goblins weren't evil to begin with. They were corrupted. I've never had those sorts of feelings about the Germans. I'm very anti that kind of thing."

Students produce lots of allegories. They suggest that the Dark Lord's ring represents the Bomb, and the goblins, the Russians. Or, more cheekily, that Treebeard, the tall, treelike being, "his eyes filled with age and long, slow, steady thinking," is Tolkien himself. In a rather portly note to his publishers, he replied: "It is not about anything but itself. (Certainly it has *no* allegorical intentions, general, particular, or topical, moral, religious or political.)" But he will agree that the Shire, the agreeable hobbit country, is like the West Midlands he remembers: "It provides a fairly good living with moderately good husbandry and is tucked away from all centers of disturbance; it comes to be regarded as divinely protected, though people there didn't realize it at the time. That's rather how England used to be, isn't it?"

Except for five years at Leeds University, where he was Professor of English Language from 1924 to 1925, Tolkien spent the rest of his life in Oxford. He wrote his earliest stories and verse there, and was often seen riding a rather old bicycle. Another don was mildly surprised one day, after Tolkien began to receive royalties from his books, to see him in a Daimler. Nowadays, a hired car sometimes goes shopping for him. He gets up at 8:30 in the morning and goes to bed at 2 A.M. How does he spend his days? Tolkien has a small, exploding laugh. "Working like hell. A pen is to me as a beak is to a hen."

He says he's no storyteller, but all the same, Tolkien would rather enjoy making a recording of his work, doing all the different voices: rustic ones for the hobbits and a horrid, high, hissing one for Gollum, the creature who slithers after them, trying to win back the Dark Lord's ring for himself. The BBC has dramatized Tolkien with a cast including Tom Forrest of *The Archers*. Tolkien says, "I've a very strong visual imagination, but it's not so strong in other points. I doubt if many authors visualize very closely faces and voices. If you write a long story like *The Lord of the Rings*, you've got to write it twice over, and you end up writing it backwards, of course. People will occur. One waits to see what's coming next. I knew there was going to be some trouble with treelike creatures at one point or another.

"A lot of the criticism of the verses shows a complete failure to understand the fact that they are all dramatic verses: they were conceived as the kind of things people would say under the circumstances." Tolkien's books run with poetry; tinkling poems, harsh and gloomy ones, they can be extremely affable or extremely primitive. Donald Swann has put six of them to music (he says *The Lord of the Rings* got into his blood and he now reads it every spring). One of the songs is actually sung in Elvish. Tolkien sent instructions to the singer on how to sound the words, stressing that he must roll his *r*'s.

Swann first presented the songs to Tolkien at a private party last March in Merton College to celebrate his golden wedding. Afterwards, Tolkien bowed and said, "The words are unworthy of the music."

If it had been left to him, he would have written all of his books in Elvish. "The invention of language is the foundation," he says. "The stories were made rather to provide a world for the language than the reverse. To me a name comes first and the story follows. But, of course, such a work as *The*

Lord of the Rings has been edited, and only as much language has been left in as I thought would be stomached by readers. I now find that many would have liked much more." In America especially, Tolkien words are creeping into everyday usage; for example, *mathom*, meaning an article one saves but doesn't use. A senior girl at the Bronx High School of Science says, "I wrote my notes in Elvish. Even now, I doodle in Elvish. It's my means of expression."

What does Tolkien think of that? Does he like Americans? "I don't like anyone very much in that sense. I'm against generalizations." One persists. Does he like Americans? "Art moves them and they don't know what they've been moved by and they get quite drunk on it," Tolkien says. "Many young Americans are involved in the stories in a way that I am not.

"But they do use this sometimes as a means against some abomination. There was one campus, I forget which, where the council of the university pulled down a very pleasant little grove of trees to make way for what they called a 'Culture Center' out of some sort of concrete blocks. The students were outraged. They wrote 'another bit of Mordor' on it."

England has not such a spreading, reveling Tolkien cult. There are middle-aged graduates who were transfixed (as the poet W. H. Auden was) by the beautiful way the professor could read from a dusty work like *Beowulf,* and there are the smart children interested by slightly difficult styles. In England, Tolkien is a leisurely word-of-mouth craze.

But at the Berkeley campus bookstore, Fred Cody, the manager, said, "This is more than a campus craze; it's like a drug dream." In the United States hobbits have quite replaced Salinger and Golding as "in" reading. Tolkien seems to promote a mild kind of intellectual hooliganism. But his supporters argue (overwhelmingly) that, on the contrary, it does everyone good to stay in the Tolkien world, where things are still green; there is hope for people and pleasantness. At Ballantine Books, the paperback company which publishes

Tolkien, an editor thought that "young people today are interested in power, and they are interested in working out the conflict of good and evil. Here it is worked out for them."

If that sounds overly simple and sententious, consider the point C. S. Lewis once made, asking why Tolkien should have chosen to point morals in such an extravagant fantasy:

"Because, I take it . . . the real life of men is of that mythical and heroic quality. . . . The imagined beings have their inside on the outside; they are visible souls. And Man as a whole, Man pitted against the Universe, have we seen him at all till we see that he is like a hero in a fairy tale?"

That is one quality with a powerful appeal to students. There is another. Tolkien's writings allow thousands into the finest and most select kind of college tutorial; they demand that attention be paid. J.I.M. Stewart, another Oxford don storyteller—he writes detective stories as Michael Innes—puts the thing perfectly in his memory of Tolkien as an orator. "He could turn a lecture room into a mead hall in which he was the bard and we were the feasting, listening guests."

—*The New York Times Magazine*, January 15, 1967

Interview with Tom Shippey

Author of J.R.R. Tolkien: Author of the Century

The following interview with Tom Shippey was conducted by Houghton Mifflin in May 2001.

Why do you call Tolkien "author of the century"?

Two reasons: First, he has consistently won what you might call the popular vote, in readers' polls for their favorite book or the one they've found most influential. Second, although he seems on the face of it to be an antiquarian author writing about an imaginary far past, I am convinced that the reason he consistently wins the polls is that his work articulates some of the deepest and most specific concerns of the twentieth century—concerns such as industrialized warfare, the temptations of power, the origins of evil, the failure of good intentions and righteous causes.

Why do you think Tolkien has been so popular with readers?

He opened up a new imaginative space—he would have said that it was an old imaginative space, which had been walled off, that of traditional legend and fairy-tale, but I would say that he did something new with it, which was to provide a world of dwarves and trolls and elves and wizards (and so on)—with a map, with a consistent history and geography, which feels as if it is indefinitely extendable. That's why there have been so many successors to Tolkien, writing fantasy trilogies or sequences of the same types, maps included.

The other and deeper reason is that he answers questions that have deeply preoccupied ordinary people, but that have not been answered by the official (or self-elected) speakers of our culture—writers, politicians, philosophers. The most obvious one is, Why has the twentieth century been so unremittingly evil? The nineteenth century was looking forward to moral progress and freedom from want. Where (in Tolkien's lifetime and mine) did it all go wrong? I think his images of evil, like the Ringwraiths, are at the same time completely original, highly contemporary, and mythically timeless. What they say is that anyone can turn into a wraith, and you can't be sure when it will start. Nor can you deal with evil just by being a nice guy yourself. It may force itself upon you. Tolkien's images of good are similarly mixed, complicated, and satisfying. His work has great emotional depth.

So why has Tolkien been so unpopular with the critics?

They sense a challenge to the dominant literary orthodoxy of the past century, which has been ironic and self-doubting. I see this as a legacy of World War I, the Great War, which destroyed traditional certainties and traditional authorities. Tolkien was himself a combat veteran of that war, and I would regard him as one of the rather large group of "traumatized authors" writing fantasy (Orwell, Golding, Vonnegut, etc.), but his experience made him want to restate traditional images rather than throw them away. In particular he wanted to find a new way to represent heroes and heroism. He knew the old ways very well, and he knew they wouldn't work anymore, but he did not want to abandon the effort. This essentially positive and optimistic view of humanity (and nonhumanity) has been dismissed as shallow and unthinking, but that is a bad mistake. Tolkien knew much more about irony than any of his critics, and about war.

How do these affect one's view of Tolkien the man?

They bring out his inner anxieties. One should remember that Tolkien did not get his major work into print until he was sixty-two, and that for most of his working life the chances were that he was going to remain forever unpublished. He sometimes imagines his own work surviving into the future as a single manuscript, never read by anybody, with the name of the author lost—exactly like the poem *Beowulf*, in fact. Of course his work has now sold hundreds of millions of copies, and is set to do the same again in the next generation, and *Beowulf* in the end has had more books and articles written about it than *Hamlet*. That's ironic, but not all ironies have to be negative ones.

What effect has Tolkien had on modern fantasy?

He created the genre—not quite single-handedly, but very nearly so. I discuss other fantasy traditions in my *Oxford Book of Fantasy Stories,* but the shelves in modern bookstores would look very different if Tolkien had not written, or if Stanley Unwin had decided not to publish him after all, back in the early 1950s. The eagerness with which he was followed suggests that there was a suppressed desire for the kind of thing he did, but nobody before him quite knew how to do it, or thought it was allowed. C. S. Lewis said Tolkien was as hard to influence as a bandersnatch, and only somebody like that could have broken the literary convention and establish wisdom in the way that he did.

What remains unique in Tolkien's work?

Two things I'd pick out are the poetry and the sense of shape. There are a lot of poems in *The Lord of the Rings,* in many different styles and format, and not many other fantasy writers have the confidence or the literary background to go inventing whole new poetic traditions (or reinventing old ones). But this gives Tolkien's work a mythic and imaginative dimension, which has never been duplicated. As for the shape, *The Lord of the Rings* is very tightly controlled, with multiple plots integrated by a day-to-day chronology, which you really need to follow. What it does is make each of the characters feel lonely and isolated, while in the broader view you can see that everyone's story is a part of everyone else's: much more like reality than the plot of a conventional novel. It works laterally as well as linearly.

The Critics

Kicking the Hobbit

by Chris Mooney

When it comes to the fantasy novels of J.R.R. Tolkien, it is a truism that critics either love the books or hate them: Concerning Middle Earth, there is no middle ground. Such has been the case ever since Tolkien, an Oxford philologist, first published his epic novel *The Lord of the Rings* in three volumes (*The Fellowship of the Ring, The Two Towers,* and *The Return of the King*) between 1954 and 1955. In 1956 W. H. Auden wrote in *The New York Times* that, in some respects, Tolkien's story of the hobbit Frodo's quest to destroy the Dark Lord Sauron's "One Ring" of power surpassed even Milton's *Paradise Lost.* But that same year, Edmund Wilson, at the time America's preeminent man of letters, dismissed *The Lord of the Rings* as "balderdash" in a review for *The Nation* titled "Ooh, Those Awful Orcs." Wilson also swatted at Tolkien defenders like Auden and C. S. Lewis, observing that "certain people—especially, perhaps, in Britain—have a life-long appetite for juvenile trash."

Wilson's derisive review inaugurated an estimable tradition of hobbit bashing, but the enduring success of Tolkien's fiction has bedeviled his literary detractors. In 1961 Philip Toynbee wrote optimistically in *The Observer* of London that Tolkien's works had "passed into a merciful oblivion." Forty years later, *The Lord of the Rings* has sold 50 million copies in numerous languages, influencing everything from *Star Wars* to Led Zeppelin and single-handedly spawning the genre of fantasy fiction in the process. (Tolkien's 1937 novel, *The Hobbit,* has sold almost as many copies.) These days, Tolkien fans are counting down the weeks until December, when *The Fellowship of the Ring,* the first of New Line Cinema's three projected Tolkien blockbusters, is to appear in theaters.

In Britain, Tolkien's literary merits have been the subject of very public debate. In 1996 a poll of 26,000 readers by Waterstone's bookstore crowned *The Lord of the Rings* "book of the century." Writing in *W: The Waterstone's Magazine,* Germaine Greer expressed her displeasure at the poll results.

> Ever since I arrived at Cambridge as a student in 1964 and encountered a tribe of full-grown women wearing puffed sleeves, clutching teddies and babbling excitedly about the doings of hobbits, it has been my nightmare that Tolkien would turn out to be the most influential writer of the twentieth century. The bad dream has materialised.

In his curt introduction to last year's Chelsea House critical edition *J.R.R. Tolkien's "The Lord of the Rings,"* Harold Bloom—the famously Falstaffian Yale English prof who has designated himself the gatekeeper of the Western literary canon—calls Tolkien's romance "inflated, over-written, tendentious, and moralistic in the extreme." Bloom concludes: "Whether [Tolkien] is an author for the coming century seems to me open to some doubt."

Yet the very fact that Harold Bloom has edited two books of Tolkien criticism suggests that *The Lord of the Rings* may be on the verge of some form of canonicity. There's certainly enough Tolkien scholarship out there to sustain that. Tolkien's phalanx of adoring literary defenders insist that his story of hobbits and Middle Earth is an outstanding, original, and, above all, thoroughly modern literary work that has been unjustly maligned by snobbish literati.

Though still marginal in the academy, the Tolkienists may

be gaining ground. In May [2001] Houghton Mifflin published *J.R.R. Tolkien: Author of the Century,* a comprehensive defense of Tolkien's fiction by St. Louis University professor T.A. Shippey. Shippey is a serious scholar, and in fact has held the very chair of English language and medieval literature at Leeds University that Tolkien vacated in 1925. Shippey's book was released a year ago in the United Kingdom and sparked some typically vituperative debate: One reviewer dismissed it as "a belligerently argued piece of fan-magazine polemic."

Earlier in the month, the Medieval Institute at Western Michigan University in Kalamazoo—whose annual meeting is ground zero for professional medievalists—devoted three full sessions to Tolkien for the first time. Tolkien's scholarship has long appealed to medievalists; his famous 1936 essay *"Beowulf:* The Monster and the Critics"was recently anointed by Harvard University poet (and *Beowulf* translator) Seamus Heaney as the "one publication that stands out" in *Beowulf* criticism."People are starting to take Tolkien seriously," says University of Maryland English professor Verlyn Flieger, a presenter in Kalamazoo who has published two books on Tolkien."He's been dead long enough."

In some ways, Tolkien scholarship resembles scholarship on James Joyce, say, or William Faulkner. Critics pore over Tolkien's correspondence and unpublished papers and sketches—many of which have been posthumously released by his son and literary executor Christopher Tolkien—for clues into the writer's mind and imagined universe. There are Tolkien biographies and bibliographies; there are Tolkien-studies organizations; there are university-based Tolkienists as well as numerous independent ones.

Not unlike what has happened with Joyce, the line between Tolkien scholarship and Tolkien fandom can get rather blurry. Consider Rice University English professor Jane Chance, who organized the Kalamazoo Tolkien panels, has published two books on Tolkien, and teaches "English

318: J.R.R. Tolkien." The syllabus sounds like many other colleges lit classes: "The course will trace the tension between the exile ... and the community, otherness and heroism, identity and marginalization, revenge and forgiveness."

But when I asked Chance what it's like teaching Tolkien, her response was startling: "I can only speak very personally, from having taught Shakespeare and Tolkien: I don't see any difference." Certainly, *The Lord of the Rings* is a rich and multilayered text; its author was a man of deep learning and imagination who created a mind-bogglingly vast and detailed fictional world, complete with its own history, civilizations, and languages. Touring Middle Earth with Tolkien can be like touring the Mediterranean with Herodotus. Still, when Tolkienists claim "author of the century" honors and swing for the fences by comparing their man to the Bard, it's small wonder that the likes of Harold Bloom are withholding their seal of approval.

Morever, part of the trouble for some of Tolkien's more jaundiced critics is the political culture that surrounds him. Certain detractors, like Greer, cannot forget the 1960s, when "Frodo Lives!" graffiti and T-shirts abounded. Despite Tolkien's conservative—some would say reactionary—Catholic politics, *The Lord of the Rings* became required reading for counterculturists during the Vietnam era. In the wizard Gandalf's counsel that the powerful but corrupting Ring be destroyed, rather than used as a weapon against Sauron, antiwar activists saw a clear allusion to the scourge of nuclear weapons. Environmentalists, meanwhile, pointed to Tolkien's beloved Ents, the ruminative tree-creatures who are "roused" to protect their forest of Fangorn from the ax-loving wizard Saruman—who, with his "mind of metal and wheels ... does not care for growing things, except as far as they serve him for the moment." And then there are the hobbits' frequent time-outs to enjoy mushrooms and "pipe weed." Pot smokers felt they knew exactly what Tolkien was driving at.

Tolkien himself was no fan of these fans, some of whom to

this day take his famous comment "I am in fact a hobbit" as an invitation to get together and dress up as characters from the novel. David Bratman, former editor of the Tolkien studies newsletter *Mythprints,* says Tolkien's "deplorable cultus" (in the author's own words) should not be held against him. "Artists should not be blamed for attracting a following of fools," concurred another British critic in 1992, "—or if they should, we should downgrade Blake, Byron, and D. H. Lawrence."

Elf-besotted fans aside, why shouldn't Tolkien be granted admission to the literary pantheon? Well, for one thing, his detractors argue, his prose is unbearably archaic. "Sometimes, reading Tolkien, I am reminded of the Book of Mormon," writes Bloom. Tolkien's verse—which litters the text of *The Lord of the Rings*—is generally accepted to be even worse.

But the critical objections to *The Lord of the Rings* aren't merely stylistic; many find Tolkien's sensibilities to be premodernist, even retrograde. Tolkien's worldview was hardly forward-looking. On the contrary, his youthful traumas in World War I left him reclusive and devoutly antimodern for the rest of his life. "One has indeed personally to come under the shadow of war to feel its oppression," wrote Tolkien. "By 1918 all but one of my close friends were dead." And so Tolkien buried himself in the study of ancient languages and the construction of a theory of fantasy—expounded in his influential essay "On Fairy Stories"—emphasizing its power to access profound and perhaps mythic realities beneath the surface of everyday life.

Again and again, this theory—and the literature that is supposed to embody it—has been derided as escapist. Thus, the burden has tended to rest with Tolkienists to show that despite his archaisms, Tolkien was nevertheless a modern author. Shippey, for example, sees *The Lord of the Rings* as an unfailingly modern work in its attempt, through the fantasy mode, to grapple with the greatest trauma of the twentieth century: the evidence of radical human evil presented by the two world wars. During the siege of the city of Minas Tirith by the forces of Mordor in *The Return of the King*, Tolkien presents this scene of a catapult volley:

> All about the streets and lanes behind the Gate it tumbled down, small round shot that did not burn. But when men ran to learn what it might be, they cried aloud or wept. For the enemy was flinging into the City all the heads of those who had fallen fighting.... They were grim to look on; for though some were crushed and shapeless, and some had been cruelly hewn, yet many had features that could be told, and it seemed that they had died in pain.

Though this rain of heads takes place in a fantasy world, the sense of the brutally horrific conveys Tolkien's experience as a World War I trench veteran. Indeed, Shippey groups Tolkien with George Orwell, Kurt Vonnegut, and William Golding as authors who turned to fantasy or imagined worlds in order to grapple with traumatic war experiences. Neither *1984* nor *Animal Farm*—which occupied second and third place, respectively, behind *The Lord of the Rings* in the Waterstone poll—could be described as works of literary "realism." Yet we accept both as deeply serious and political responses to Orwell's experiences of fascism and communism.

Tolkien claimed that he never stooped to allegory in his writings, but he did not deny "applicability." Thus, *The Lord of the Rings* can be read as his response to modernity, to the world of catastrophic wars, terrible weapons, and industrialization that Tolkien felt was destroying his beloved rural, Edwardian England (represented in his books by the hobbits' peaceful, if parochial, homeland of "the Shire"). And if Tolkien's One Ring represents technology, or humanity's hubristic capacity to tamper with nature, then the message is: Destroy it forever.

Some scholars see in Tolkien's strongly anti-technology

views a powerful enviro-Luddite strain. In his 1997 book *Defending Middle Earth: Tolkien, Myth, and Modernity*, Patrick Curry treats Tolkien as a kind of Green movement precursor—a literary Lorax. "In all my works I take the part of trees as against all their enemies," Tolkien wrote in 1972. But there's more than just an admiration of nature in Tolkien; there's the converse, a deep distrust of all things "unnatural." When the wizard Saruman presumes to tinker with nature, the Ent Treebeard reacts by saying, "That would be a black evil!" The Jeremy Rifkins and Kirkpatrick Sales of the world—along with other opponents of human-genome research, cloning, and biotechnology—would find a kindred spirit in Tolkien. So, for that matter, would the Unabomber.

But probably the main reason Tolkien has not been accepted by most critics is that his writings do not conform to the tenets of literary modernism. Tolkien's language largely eschews irony, his imagery tends to be generic, and, with some exceptions, his characters go unexplored. In *Aspects of the Novel*, E. M. Forster's blueprint of modernist literary theory, story and plot are gently derided. But in *The Lord of the Rings*, plot is probably the most compelling literary element. Readers steeped in modernist literature simply don't know how to respond to Tolkien's prose.

They also have trouble understanding Tolkien's philological approach: He studied literature and the history of languages with equal emphasis. Tolkien once wrote of his novels that "the invention of languages is the foundation. . . . To me a name comes first and the story follows." Reading this, critics have understandably accused Tolkien of swapping word games for the composition of literature. Shippey observes sadly that this is simply because in the battle for ascendancy among competing literary paradigms within the academy, philology lost out.

> It is now very hard to pursue a course of philology of the kind Tolkien would have approved in any British or American university. The misologists won, in the academic world; as did the realists, the modernists, the post-modernists, the despisers of fantasy.
>
> But they lost outside the academic world....

And this is what Tolkienists cling to. In celebrating Tolkien's enduring bestsellerdom, they implicitly claim a popular mandate to retrieve from the past the values, academic modes, and literary tastes that would allow us to better appreciate his writings. And yet given his sweeping attack on modernity, it may be that the case for Tolkien as a writer for this century must inevitably fail.

Still, Tolkienists have the staggering popularity of *The Lord of the Rings* on their side—a key factor in the literary reputation of Charles Dickens, for example. Some Tolkienists observe knowingly that the upcoming films will no doubt hook the Harry Potter generation on *The Lord of the Rings* (though purists may secretly be a bit nervous about Hobbit Happy Meals). Meanwhile, Tolkien criticism is already a substantial body of work, much of which cannot be dismissed outright as fan pamphleteering. When it comes to Tolkien, says Jane Chance, "the popular has become canonical"—or at any rate, it is becoming more and more so. Ultimately, Tolkien's literary stature may be assured by sheer momentum.

—*The American Prospect,* June 4, 2001

The Gods Return to Earth

C. S. Lewis

T*he Fellowship of the Ring* is like lightning from a clear sky; as sharply different, as unpredictable in our age as *Songs of Innocence* were in theirs. To say that in it heroic romance, gorgeous, eloquent, and unashamed, has suddenly returned at a period almost pathological in its anti-romanticism, is inadequate. To us, who live in that odd period, the return—and the sheer relief of it—is doubtless the important thing. But in the history of Romance itself—a history which stretches back to *The Odyssey* and beyond—it makes not a return but an advance or revolution: the conquest of new territory.

Nothing quite like it was ever done before. "One takes it," says Naomi Mitchison, "as seriously as Malory." But then the ineluctable sense of reality which we feel in the *Morte d'Arthur* comes largely from the great weight of other men's work built up century by century, which has gone into it. The utterly new achievement of Professor Tolkien is that he carries a comparable sense of reality unaided. Probably no book yet written in the world is quite such a radical instance of what its author has elsewhere called "sub-creation." The direct debt (there are of course subtler kinds of debt) which every author must owe to the actual universe is here deliberately reduced to the minimum. Not content to create his own story, he creates, with an almost insolent prodigality, the whole world in which it is to

move, with its own theology, myths, geography, history, pale-
ography, languages, and orders of beings—a world "full of
strange creatures beyond count." The names alone are a feast,
whether redolent of quiet countryside (Michel Delving,
South Farthing), tall and kingly (Boromir, Faramir, Elendil),
loathsome like Sméagol, who is also Gollum, or frowning in
the evil strength of Barad-dûr or Gorgoroth; yet best of all
(Lothlórien, Gilthoniel, Galadriel) when they embody that
piercing, high elvish beauty of which no other prose writer
has captured so much.

Such a book has of course its predestined readers, even
now more numerous and more critical than is always realized.
To them a reviewer need say little, except that here are beau-
ties which pierce like swords or burn like cold iron; here is a
book that will break your heart. They will know that this is
good news, good beyond hope. To complete their happiness
one need only add that it promises to be gloriously long: this
volume is only the first of three. But it is too great a book to
rule only its natural subjects. Something must be said to
"those without," to the unconverted. At the very least, possible misunderstandings may be got out of the way.

First, we must clearly understand that though *The
Fellowship* in one way continues its author's fairy tale, *The
Hobbit,* it is in no sense an overgrown "juvenile." The truth is
the other way round. *The Hobbit* was merely a fragment torn
from the author's huge myth and adapted for children:
inevitably losing something by the adaptation. *The Fellowship*
gives us at last the lineaments of that myth "in their true
dimensions like themselves." Misunderstanding on this point
might easily be encouraged by the first chapter, in which the
author (taking a risk) writes almost in the manner of the earlier and far lighter book. With some who will find the main
body of the book deeply moving, this chapter may not be a
favourite.

Yet there were good reasons for such an opening, still
more for the Prologue (wholly admirable, this) which pre-

cedes it. It is essential that we should first be well steeped in the "homeliness," the frivolity, even (in its best sense) the vulgarity of the creatures called Hobbits; these unambitious folk, peaceable yet almost anarchical, with faces "good-natured rather than beautiful" and "mouths apt to laughter and eating," who treat smoking as an art and like books which tell them what they already know. They are not an allegory of the English, but they are perhaps a myth that only an Englishman (or, should we add, a Dutchman?) could have created. Almost the central theme of the book is the contrast between the Hobbits (or "the Shire") and the appalling destiny to which some of them are called, the terrifying discovery that the humdrum happiness of the Shire, which they had taken for granted as something normal, is in reality a sort of local and temporary accident, that its existence depends on being protected by powers which Hobbits forget against powers which Hobbits dare not imagine, that any Hobbit may find himself forced out of the Shire and caught up into that high conflict. More strangely still, the event of that conflict between strongest things may come to depend on him, who is almost the weakest.

What shows that we are reading myth, not allegory, is that there are no pointers to a specifically theological or political, or psychological application. A myth points, for each reader, to the realm he lives in most. It is a master key; use it on what door you like. And there are other themes in *The Fellowship* equally serious.

That is why no catchwords about "escapism" or "nostalgia" and no distrust of "private worlds" are in court. This is no Angria, no dreaming; it is sane and vigilant invention, revealing at point after point the integration of the author's mind. What is the use of calling "private" a world all walk into and test and in which we find such a balance? As for escapism, what we chiefly escape is the illusions of our ordinary life. We certainly do not escape anguish. Despite many a snug fireside and many an hour of good cheer to gratify the Hobbit in each of us, anguish is, for me, almost the prevailing note. But not, as in the literature most typical of our age, the anguish of abnormal or contorted souls: rather that anguish of those who were happy before a certain darkness came up and will be happy if they live to see it gone.

Nostalgia does indeed come in; not ours nor the author's, but that of the characters. It is closely connected with one of Professor Tolkien's greatest achievements. One would have supposed that diuturnity was the quality least likely to be found in an invented world. And one has, in fact, an uneasy feeling that the worlds of the *Furioso* or *The Water of the Wondrous Isles* weren't there at all before the curtain rose. But in the Tolkienian world you can hardly put your foot down anywhere from Esgaroth to Forlindon or between Ered Mithrin and Khand, without stirring the dust of history. Our own world, except at certain rare moments, hardly seems so heavy with its past. This is one element in the anguish which the characters bear. But with the anguish there comes also a strange exaltation. They are at once stricken and upheld by the memory of vanished civilizations and lost splendor. They have outlived the second and third Ages; the wine of life was drawn long since. As we read we find ourselves sharing their burden; when we have finished, we return to our own life not relaxed but fortified.

But there is more in the book still. Every now and then, risen from sources we can only conjecture and almost alien (one would think) to the author's habitual imagination, figures meet us so brimming with life (not human life) that they make our sort of anguish and our sort of exaltation seem unimportant. Such is Tom Bombadil, such the unforgettable Ents. This is surely the utmost reach of invention, when an author produces what seems to be not even his own, much less anyone else's. Is mythopoeia, after all, not the most, but the least, subjective of activities?

Even now I have left out almost everything—the silvan leafiness, the passions, the high virtues, the remote horizons.

Even if I had space I could hardly convey them. And after all, the most obvious appeal of the book is perhaps also its deepest: "there was sorrow then too, and gathering dark, but great valour, and great deeds that were not wholly vain." *Not wholly vain*—it is the cool middle point between illusion and disillusionment.

—*Time and Tide*, August 14, 1954

Oo, Those Awful Orcs!

by Edmund Wilson

In 1937, Dr. J.R.R. Tolkien, an Oxford don, published a children's book called *The Hobbit,* which had an immense success. The hobbits are a not quite human race who inhabit an imaginary country called the Shire and who combine the characteristics of certain English animals—they live in burrows like rabbits and badgers—with the traits of English country-dwellers, ranging from rustic to tweedy. (The name seems a telescoping of rabbit and Hobbs.) They have elves, trolls and dwarfs as neighbors, and they are associated with a magician called Gandalf and a slimy water creature called Gollum. Dr. Tolkien became interested in his fairy-tale country and has gone on from this little story to elaborate a long romance, which has appeared under the general title *The Lord of the Rings,* in three volumes: *The Fellowship of the Ring, The Two Towers* and *The Return of the King.* All volumes are accompanied with maps, and Dr. Tolkien, who is a philologist, professor of English Language and Literature at Merton College, has equipped the last volume with a scholarly apparatus of appendices, explaining the alphabets and grammars of the various tongues spoken by his characters, and giving full genealogies and tables of historical chronology.

Dr. Tolkien has announced that this series—the hypertrophic sequel to *The Hobbit*—is intended for adults rather than children, and it has had a resounding reception at the

hands of a number of critics who are certainly grown-up in
years. Mr. Richard Hughes, for example, has written of it that
nothing of the kind on such a scale has been attempted since
The Faerie Queen, and that "for width of imagination it almost
beggars parallel." "It's odd, you know," says Miss Naomi
Mitchison, "one takes it as seriously as Malory." And Mr. C. S.
Lewis, also of Oxford, is able to top them all: "If Ariosto," he
ringingly writes, "rivalled it in invention (in fact, he does not),
he would still lack its heroic seriousness." Nor has America
been behind. In the *Saturday Review of Literature,* a Mr. Louis
J. Halle, author of a book on civilization and foreign policy,
answers as follows a lady who—"lowering," he says, "her
pince-nez"—has inquired what he finds in Tolkien: "What,
dear lady, does this invented world have to do with our own?
You ask for its meaning—as you ask for meaning of *The
Odyssey,* of *Genesis,* of *Faust*—in a word? In a word, then, its
meaning is 'heroism.' It makes our own world, once more,
heroic. What higher meaning than this is to be found in any
literature?"

But if one goes from these eulogies to the book itself, one
is likely to be let down, astonished, baffled. This reviewer has
just read the whole thing aloud to his seven-year-old daughter, who has been through *The Hobbit* countless times, beginning it again the moment she has finished, and whose interest
has been held by its more prolix successors. One is puzzled to
know why the author should have supposed he was writing
for adults. There are, to be sure, some details that are a little
unpleasant for a children's book, but except when he is being
pedantic and also boring the adult reader, there is little in *The
Lord of the Rings* over the head of a seven-year-old child. It is
essentially a children's book—a children's book which has
somehow got out of hand, instead of directing it at the "juvenile" market, the author has indulged himself in developing
the fantasy for its own sake; and it ought to be said at this
point, before emphasizing its inadequacies as literature, that
Dr. Tolkien makes few claims for his fairy romance. In a state-

ment prepared for his publishers, he has explained that he began it to amuse himself, as a philological game: "The invention of languages is the foundation. The 'stories' were made rather to provide a world for the languages than the reverse. I should have preferred to write in 'Elvish.'" He has omitted, he says, in the printed book, a good deal of the philological part; "but there is a great deal of linguistic matter ... included or mythologically expressed in the book. It is to me, anyway, largely an essay in 'linguistic esthetic,' as I sometimes say to people who ask me 'what it is all about.' . . . It is not 'about' anything but itself. Certainly it has *no* allegorical intentions, general, particular, or topical, moral, religious, or political." An overgrown fairy story, a philological curiosity—that is, then, what *The Lord of the Rings* really is. The pretentiousness is all on the part of Dr. Tolkien's infatuated admirers, and it is these pretensions that I would here assail.

The most distinguished of Tolkien's admirers and the most conspicuous of his defenders has been Mr. W. H. Auden. That Auden is a master of English verse and a well-equipped critic of verse, no one, as they say, will dispute. It is significant, then, that he comments on the badness of Tolkien's verse—there is a great deal of poetry in *The Lord of the Rings*. Mr. Auden is apparently quite insensitive—through lack of interest in the other department—to the fact that Tolkien's prose is just as bad. Prose and verse are on the same level of professorial amateurishness. What I believe has misled Mr. Auden is his own special preoccupation with the legendary theme of the Quest. He has written a book about the literature of the Quest; he has experimented with the theme himself in a remarkable sequence of sonnets; and it is to be hoped that he will do something with it on an even larger scale. In the meantime—as sometimes happens with works that fall in with one's interests—he no doubt so overrates *The Lord of the Rings* because he reads into it something that he means to write himself. It is indeed the tale of a Quest, but, to the reviewer, an extremely unrewarding one. The hero has no serious temptations; is lured by no insidious enchantments, perplexed by few problems. What we get is a simple confrontation—in more or less the traditional terms of British melodrama—of the Forces of Evil with the Forces of Good, the remote and alien villain with the plucky little home-grown hero. There are streaks of imagination: the ancient tree-spirits, the Ents, with their deep eyes, twiggy beards, rumbly voices; the Elves, whose nobility and beauty is elusive and not quite human. But even these are rather clumsily handled. There is never much development in the episodes; you simply go on getting more of the same thing. Dr. Tolkien has little skill at narrative and no instinct for literary form. The characters talk in story-book language that might have come out of Howard Pyle, and as personalities they do not impose themselves. At the end of this long romance, I had still no conception of the wizard Gandalf, who is a cardinal figure, had never been able to visualize him at all. For the most part such characterizations as Dr. Tolkien is able to contrive are perfectly stereotyped: Frodo the good little Englishman; Samwise, the doglike servant, who talks lower-class and respectful, and never deserts his master. These characters who are no characters are involved in interminable adventures the poverty of invention displayed in which is, it seems to me, almost pathetic. On the country in which the Hobbits, the Elves, the Ents and the other Good People live, the Forces of Evil are closing in, and they have to band together to save it. The hero is the Hobbit called Frodo, who has become possessed of a ring that Sauron, the King of the Enemy, wants (that learned reptilian suggestion—doesn't it give you a goosefleshy feeling?). In spite of the author's disclaimer, the struggle for the ring does seem to have some larger significance. This ring, if one continues to carry it, confers upon one special powers, but it is felt to become heavier and heavier; it exerts on one a sinister influence that one has to brace oneself to resist. The problem is for Frodo to get rid of it before he can succumb to this influence.

Now, this situation does create interest; it does seem to have possibilities. One looks forward to a queer dilemma, a new kind of hairbreadth escape, in which Frodo, in the Enemy's kingdom, will find himself half seduced into taking over the enemy's point of view, so that the realm of shadows and horrors will come to seem to him, once he is in it, once he is strong in the power of the ring, a plausible and pleasant place, and he will narrowly escape the danger of becoming a monster himself. But these bugaboos are not magnetic; they are feeble and rather blank; one does not feel they have any real power. The Good People simply say "Boo" to them. There are Black Riders, of whom everyone is terrified but who never seem anything but specters. There are dreadful hovering birds—think of it: horrible birds of prey! There are ogreish, disgusting Orcs, who, however, rarely get to the point of committing any overt acts. There is a giant female spider—a dreadful creepy-crawly spider!—who lives in a dark cave and eats people. What one misses in all these terrors is any trace of concrete reality. The preternatural, to be effective, should be given some sort of solidity, a real presence, recognizable features—like Gulliver, like Gogol, like Poe; not like those phantom horrors of Algernon Blackwood, which prove also disappointing after the travel-book substantiality of the landscapes in which he evokes them. Tolkien's horrors resemble these in their lack of real contact with their victims, who dispose of them as we do of the horrors in dreams by simply pushing them or pulling them away. As for Sauron, the ruler of Mordor (doesn't the very name have a shuddery sound?), who concentrates in his person everything that is threatening the Shire, the buildup for him goes on through three volumes. He makes his first, rather promising, appearance as a terrible fire-rimmed yellow eye seen in a water-mirror. But this is as far as we ever get. Once Sauron's realm is invaded, we think we are going to meet him; but he still remains nothing but a burning eye scrutinizing all that occurs from the window of a remote dark tower. This might, of course, be made effective; but actually it is not; we never feel Sauron's power. And the climax to which we have been working up through exactly nine hundred and ninety-nine large, close-printed pages, when it comes, proves extremely flat. The ring is at last got rid of by being dropped into a fiery crater, and the kingdom of Sauron "topples" in a brief and banal earthquake that sets fire to everything and burns it up, and so releases the author from the necessity of telling the reader what exactly was so terrible there. Frodo has come to the end of his Quest, but the reader has remained untouched by the wounds and fatigues of his journey. An impotence of imagination seems to me to sap the whole story. The wars are never dynamic; the ordeals give no sense of strain; the fair ladies would not stir a heartbeat; the horrors would not hurt a fly.

Now, how is it that these long-winded volumes of what looks to this reviewer like balderdash have elicited such tributes as those above? The answer is, I believe, that certain people—especially, perhaps, in Britain, have a lifelong appetite for juvenile trash. They would not accept adult trash, but, confronted with the pre-teen-age article, they revert to the mental phase which delighted in *Elsie Dinsmore* and *Little Lord Fauntleroy* and which seems to have made of Billy Bunter, in England, almost a national figure. You can see it in the tone they fall into when they talk about Tolkien in print: they bubble, they squeal, they coo; they go on about Malory and Spenser—both of whom have a charm and a distinction that Tolkien has never touched.

As for me, if we must read about imaginary kingdoms, give me James Branch Cabell's Poictesme. He at least writes for grown-up people, and he does not present the drama of life as a showdown between Good People and Goblins. He can cover more ground in an episode that lasts only three pages than Tolkien is able to in one of his twenty-page chapters, and he can create a more disquieting impression by a reference to something that is never described than Tolkien through his whole demonology.

—*The Nation*, April 14, 1956

THE STARING EYE

by Ursula K. Le Guin

They were displayed on the new aquisitions rack of the university library: three handsome books, in the Houghton Mifflin edition, with beige and black dust jackets, each centered with a staring black and red Eye.

Sometimes one, or two, or all three of them were out; sometimes all three were there together. I was aware of them every time I was in the library, which was often. I was uneasily aware of them. They stared at me.

The *Saturday Review* had run a special notice upon the publication of the last volume, praising the work with uncharacteristic vigor and conviction. I had thought then, I must have a look at this. But when it appeared in the library, I shied away from it. I was afraid of it. It looks dull, I thought—like the *Saturday Review.* It's probably affected. It's probably allegorical. Once I went so far as to pick up Volume II, when it alone was on the rack, and look at the first page. "The Two Towers." People were rushing around on a hill, looking for one another. The language looked a bit stilted. I put it back. The Eye stared through me.

I was (for reasons now obscure to me) reading all of Gissing. I think I had gone to the library to return *Born in Exile*, when I stopped to circle warily about the new acquisitions rack, and there they were again, all three volumes, staring. I had had about enough of the Grub Street Blues. Oh well, why not? I checked out Volume I and went home with it.

Next morning I was there at nine, and checked out the others. I read the three volumes in three days. Three weeks later I was still, at times, inhabiting Middle-earth: walking, like the Elves, in dreams waking, seeing both worlds at once, the perishing and the imperishable.

Tonight, eighteen years later, just before sitting down to write this, I was reading aloud to our nine-year-old. We have just arrived at the ruined gates of Isengard, and found Merry and Pippin sitting amongst the ruins having a snack and a smoke. The nine-year-old likes Merry, but doesn't much like Pippin. I never could tell them apart to that extent.

This is the third time I have read the book aloud—the nine-year-old has elder sisters, who read it now for themselves. We seem to have acquired three editions of it. I have no idea how many times I have read it myself. I reread a great deal, but have lost count only with Dickens, Tolstoy, and Tolkien.

Yet I believe that my hesitation, my instinctive distrust of those three volumes in the university library, was well founded. To put it in the book's own terms: something of great inherent power, even if wholly good in itself, may work destruction if used in ignorance, or at the wrong time. One must be ready; one must be strong enough.

I envy those who, born later than I, read Tolkien as children—my own children among them. I certainly have had no scruples about exposing them to it at a tender age, when their resistance is minimal. To have known, at age ten or thirteen, of the existence of Ents, and of Lothlórien—what luck!

But very few children (fortunately) are going to grow up to write fantastic novels; and despite my envy, I count it lucky that I, personally, did not and could not have read Tolkien before I was twenty-five. Because I really wonder if I could have handled it.

From the age of nine, I was writing fantasy, and I never wrote anything else. It wasn't in the least like anybody else's fantasy. I read whatever imaginative fiction I could get hold of then—*Astounding Stories,* and this and that: Dunsany was the master, the man with the keys to the gates of horn and ivory, so far as I knew. But I read everything else too, and by twenty-five, if I had any admitted masters or models in the art of fiction, in the craft of writing, they were Tolstoy and Dickens. But my immodesty was equaled by my evasiveness, for I had kept my imagination quite to myself. I had no models there. I never tried to write like Dunsany, not even like *Astounding,* once I was older than twelve. I had somewhere to go and, as I saw it, I had to get there by myself.

If I had known that one was there before me, one very much greater than myself, I wonder if I would have had the witless courage to go on.

By the time I read Tolkien, however, though I had not yet written anything of merit, I was old enough, and had worked long and hard enough at my craft, to be set in my ways: to know my own way. Even the sweep and force of that incredible imagination could not dislodge me from my own little rut and carry me, like Gollum, scuttling and whimpering along behind. So far as *writing* is concerned, I mean. When it comes to *reading,* there's a different matter. I open the book, the great wind blows, the Quest begins, I follow....

It is no matter of wonder that so many people are bored by, or detest, *The Lord of the Rings.* For one thing, there was the faddism of a few years ago—Go, Go, Gandalf—enough to turn anybody against it. Judged by any of the Seven Types of Ambiguity that haunt the groves of Academe, it is totally inadequate. For those who seek allegory, it must be maddening. (It must be an allegory! Of course Frodo is Christ!—Or is Gollum Christ?) For those whose grasp on reality is so tenuous that they crave ever-increasing doses of "realism" in their reading, it offers nothing—unless, perhaps, a shortcut to the loony bin. And there are many subtler reasons for disliking it; for instance the peculiar rhythm of the book, its continual alternation of distress and relief, threat, and reassurance, tension and relaxation: this rocking-horse gait (which is precisely what makes the huge book readable to a child of nine or ten) may well not suit a jet-age adult. And there's Aragorn, who is a stuffed shirt; and Sam, who keeps saying "sir" to Frodo until one begins to have mad visions of founding a Hobbit Socialist Party; and there isn't any sex. And there is the Problem of Evil, which some people think Tolkien muffs completely. Their arguments are superficially very good. They are the same arguments which Tolkien completely exploded, thereby freeing *Beowulf* forever from the dead hands of the pedants, in his brilliant 1934 article, "The Monster and the Critics"—an article which anyone who sees Tolkien as a Sweet Old Dear, by the way, would do well to read.

Those who fault Tolkien on the Problem of Evil are usually those who have an answer to the Problem of Evil—which he did not. What kind of answer, after all, is it to drop a magic ring into an imaginary volcano? No ideologues, not even religious ones, are going to be happy with Tolkien, unless they manage it by misreading him. For like all great artists he escapes ideology by being too quick for its nets, too complex for its grand simplicities, too fantastic for its rationality, too real for its generalizations. They will no more keep Tolkien labeled and pickled in a bottle than they will *Beowulf*, or the *Elder Edda*, or the *Odyssey*.

It does not seem right to grieve at the end of so fulfilled a life. Only, when we get to the end of the book, I know I will have to put on a stiff frown so that little Ted will not notice that I am in tears when I read the last lines:

> And he went on, and there was yellow light, and fire within; and the evening meal was ready, and he was expected. And Rose drew him in, and set him in his chair, and put little Elanor upon his lap.
> He drew a deep breath. "Well, I'm back," he said.

—*Vector* 66/67

The Ring of Evil

by Isaac Asimov

The occasion for the following essay [originally titled "The One Ring Is What We Make It"] was the fact that a TV version of the last part of The Lord of the Rings *trilogy was about to be shown on television. A new magazine,* Panorama, *asked me to write a commentary on the trilogy—any aspect of it I wished—so I did.*

It was written before I saw the show, since it had to be published concurrently with the showing. The essay, therefore, was not a review of the show but a discussion of one aspect of its symbolism (from my point of view).

After the essay appeared, I actually saw the TV show and I didn't like it—but that had nothing to do with what I had written.

✡

The Lord of the Rings is a three-volume epic of the battle between Good and Evil. The first volume is *The Fellowship of the Ring,* the second, *The Two Towers,* and the third is *The Return of the King.*

The canvas is broad, the characters are many, and the action is endlessly suspenseful and exciting. And the central object of the epic, about which all revolves, is the One Ring.

There are twenty rings altogether, which give power, but

Sauron, the "Dark Lord," the embodiment of Evil, the Satan figure, is the Lord of the Rings. He has made One Ring to be the master of the rest—

> *One Ring to rule them all, One Ring to find them,*
> *One Ring to bring them all and in the darkness bind them,*
> *In the Land of Mordor where the Shadows lie.*

As long as this One Ring exists, Evil cannot be defeated. Mordor is the blasted land in which Sauron rules and where everything is twisted and bent and perverted into his service. And Mordor will extend its poisoned atmosphere over all the world once the One Ring returns to Sauron.

For Sauron does not have it. In the long distant past, he lost control of it, and through a series of events, part of which are described in *The Hobbit*, a kind of children's prologue to *The Lord of the Rings*, the One Ring had fallen into the hands of Bilbo Baggins, the Hobbit of the title.

There are numerous forces trying to fight for the Good and to defeat Sauron, but of them all the Hobbits are the smallest and weakest. They are about the size of children and are as unsophisticated and simple as children. Yet it falls upon another Hobbit, named Frodo, a young cousin of Bilbo, to dispose of the One Ring and make sure that it will never again fall into the hands of Sauron.

At first as part of a small fellowship, struggling through a deadly and hostile world, and later with only the company of his faithful servant Sam, Frodo must find some way of avoiding Sauron's allies so that he might take the One Ring into Mordor itself. There, in Sauron's very lair, he must take it to Mount Doom, the seething volcano where the One Ring had been forged and in whose fires alone it could be melted and destroyed. With that destruction, if it can be carried through, Sauron's powers would end, and, for a time at any rate, Good would prevail.

What does this struggle represent? What contributed to

its construction inside Tolkien's mind? We might wonder if Tolkien himself, if he were still alive, could tell us entirely. Such literary constructions take on a life of their own, and there are never simple answers to "What does this mean?"

Tolkien was a student of the ancient Teutonic legends and one gets a feeling that the One Ring may be an echo of the Ring of the Nibelungen, and that behind Sauron is the evil and beautiful face of Loki, the traitorous Norse god of fire.

Then, too, *The Hobbit* was written in the 1930s and *The Lord of the Rings* in the 1950s. In between was World War II, and Tolkien lived through the climactic year of 1940, when Great Britain stood alone before the forces of Hitler. After all, the Hobbits are inhabitants of "the Shire," which is a transparent representation of Great Britain at its most idyllic, and behind Sauron there might be the demonic Adolf Hitler.

But then, too, there are wider symbolisms. Tom Bombadil is a mysterious character who seems to represent Nature as a whole. The treelike Ents characterize the green forests, and the Dwarves represent the mountains and the mineral world. There are the Elves, too, powerful but passé, representatives of a time passing into limbo, who will not survive even though Sauron were to be destroyed.

Always, though, we come back to the One Ring. What does it represent?

In the epic, it controls unlimited power and inspires infinite desire even though it is infinitely corrupting. Those who wear it are weighed down by it and tortured, but they can't let it go, though it erodes them, body and soul. Gandalf, who is the best and strongest of the characters in the book who fight for the Good, won't touch it, for he fears it will corrupt even him.

In the end, it falls upon Frodo, small and weak, to handle it. It corrupts and damages him, too, for when he stands on Mount Doom at last, and it will take but a flick of a finger to cast the One Ring to destruction and ensure the end of Evil, he finds he cannot do it. He has become the One Ring's slave.

(And in the end, it is Evil that destroys Evil, where Frodo the Good fails.)

What is the One Ring, then? What does it represent? What is it that is so desirable and so corrupting? What is it that can't be let go even though it is destroying us?

Well—

My wife, Janet, and I, on occasion, drive down the New Jersey Turnpike through a section of oil refineries where the tortured geometry of the structures stands against the sky, and where waste gases burn off in eternal flames, and where a stench reaches us that forces us to close the car windows. And as we approached it once, Janet rolled up the windows, sighed, and said, "Here comes Mordor."

She was right. The Mordor of *The Lord of the Rings* is the industrial world, which is slowly developing and taking over the whole planet, consuming it, poisoning it. The Elves represent the preindustrial technology that is passing from the scene. The Dwarves, the Ents, and Tom Bombadil represent the various facets of Nature that are being destroyed. And the Hobbits of the Shire represent the simple, pastoral past of humanity.

And the One Ring?

It is the lure of technology; the seduction of things done more easily; of products in greater quantity; of gadgets in tempting variety. It is gunpowder, and the automobile, and television; all the things that people snatch for if they don't have them; all the things that people can't let go once they do have them.

Can we let go? The automobile kills fifty thousand Americans every year. Can we abandon the automobile because of that? Does anyone even seriously suggest we try?

Our American way of life demands the burning of vast quantities of coal and oil that foul our air, sicken our lungs, pollute our soil and water, but can we abandon that burning? To feed the needs of our society, we need more oil than we can supply ourselves, so that we must obtain fully half from abroad. We obtain it from lands that hold us in chains in consequence and whom we dare not offend. Can we diminish our needs in order to break those chains?

We hold the One Ring, and it is destroying us and the world, and there is no Frodo to take the load of it upon himself, and there is no Mount Doom to take it to, and there are no events to insure the One Ring's destruction.

Is all this inevitable? Has Sauron won? Have the Shadows of the Land of Mordor fallen over all the world?

We might think so, if we wish to look at only the worst of the industrial world and visualize an impossible best of the preindustrial world.

But then, the happy pastoral world of the Shire never existed except in the mind of Nostalgia. There might have been a thin leaven of landowners and aristocrats who lived pleasant lives, but those lives were made pleasant only through the unremitting labors of servants, peasants, serfs, and slaves whose lives were one long brutality. Those who inherit the traditions of a ruling class (as Tolkien did) are too aware of the past pleasantness of life, and too unaware of the nightmare that filled it just beyond the borders of the manor house.

With all the miseries and terrors that industrialization has brought, it has nevertheless, *for the first time*, brought literacy and leisure to hundreds of millions; given them some share of material goods of the world, however shoddy and five-and-ten they might be; given them a chance at appreciating the arts, even if only at the level of comic book and hard rock; given them a chance at a life that has more than doubled in average length since preindustrial days.

It is easy to talk of the fifty thousand Americans (1 out of 4,400) who are killed by automobiles each year. We forget the much larger fractions of the population who were killed each year by infectious epidemics, deficiency diseases, and hormone disorders that are today thoroughly preventable or curable.

If we cannot give up the One Ring, there's a good reason

for that. If the One Ring is drawing us to our destruction, that is because we are misusing it in our greed and folly. Surely, there are ways of using it wisely. Are we so willing to despair so entirely of humanity as to deny that we can be sane and wise if we must be?

No, the One Ring is not wholly Evil. It is what we make it, and we must rescue and extend those parts of it that are Good.

—But never mind.

One can read *The Lord of the Rings* without getting lost in the symbolism. It is a fascinating adventure that doesn't get consumed with the reading. I have myself read it four times and like it better each time. I think it is about time I read it a fifth time.

And in doing so, I will take care to look upon the One Ring as—a ring.

—*Panorama,* May 1980

J.R.R. Tolkien's The Lord of the Rings:

by Harold Bloom

R oger Sale, Tolkien's best critic, is not included in this volume [*J.R.R. Tolkien's The Lord of the Rings: Modern Critical
Interpretations*] because the essay on *The Lord of the Rings* from
his book *Modern Heroism* is reprinted in full in the volume on
J.R.R. Tolkien in the Chelsea House series Modern Critical
Views. I will attempt, rather briefly, to define my aesthetic
doubts about Tolkien's trilogy by contrasting them to Sale's
shrewd defense of what he regards as Tolkien's and the pro-
tagonist Frodo Baggins's heroism.

Tolkien, at twenty-three, went off to the Western Front,
was wounded, and lost to the war nearly all his friends in his
own generation. For Sale, the trilogy is Tolkien's delayed, ulti-
mate reaction to the Great War, which decimated Great
Britain's young men. Tolkien dated his lifelong love of fairy
stories to his turning away from the War, and *The Lord of the
Rings* is a vast fairy-story.

Sale accurately observes that the trilogy purports to be a
quest but actually is a descent into hell. Whether a visionary
descent into hell can be rendered persuasively in language
that is acutely self-conscious, even arch, seems to me a hard
question. I am fond of *The Hobbit,* which is rarely pretentious,
but *The Lord of the Rings* seems to me inflated, over-written,
tendentious, and moralistic in the extreme. Is it not a giant
Period Piece?

Sale nevertheless makes quite a strong case for the trilogy, and a vast readership implicitly agrees with him. I don't

know whether Frodo Baggins breaks free and away from Tolkien's moralism to anything like the extent Sale suggests. Frodo, and Tolkien's deep creation of fairy-lore, are the strengths of the trilogy, in Sale's account.

But there is still the burden of Tolkien's style: stiff, false-archaic, overwrought, and finally a real hindrance in Volume III, *The Return of the King,* which I have had trouble rereading. At sixty-nine, I may just be too old, but here is *The Return of the King,* opened pretty much at random:

> At the doors of the Houses many were already gathered to see Aragorn, and they followed after him; and when at last he had supped, men came and prayed that he would heal their kinsmen or their friends whose lives were in peril through hurt or wound, or who lay under the Black Shadow. And Aragorn arose and went out, and he sent for the sons of Elrond, and together they labored far into the night. And word went through the city: "The King is come again indeed." And they named him Elfstone, because of the green stone that he wore, and so the name which it was foretold at his birth that he should bear was chosen for him by his own people.

I am not able to understand how a skilled and mature reader can absorb about fifteen hundred pages of this quaint stuff. Why "hurt or wound"; are they not the same? What justifies the heavy King James Bible influence upon this style? Sometimes, reading Tolkien, I am reminded of the Book of Mormon. Tolkien met a need, particularly in the early days of the Counterculture, in the later 1960s. Whether he is an author for the coming century seems to me open to some doubt.

—From *J.R.R. Tolkien's The Lord of the Rings: Modern Critical Interpretations,* 2000

The "Deplorable Cultus"

Hobbits in Hollywood

by Judith Shulevitz

If ever you need an image to illustrate the phrase "victim of one's own success," try this: John Ronald Reuel Tolkien, the tweediest and most persnickety of Oxford philologists, a translator and annotator of Old English, Old Norse and Welsh poetry, being forced to sit through a screening of the soon-to-be-released movie version of *The Lord of the Rings.* Imagine: A teenage actor playing Frodo Baggins, a hobbit fifty years old! New Zealand as a location for Middle-earth, whose geography was explicitly modeled on the hills and forests of Tolkien's beloved England! Tolkien, besides being a patriot, was a conservative Roman Catholic who never quite approved of his fans—many of them American hippies, at least in his day—let alone the industry of ancillary products that mushroomed around his work. He once despairingly described his own following as a "deplorable cultus."

Tolkien's deplorable cultus is now woven so deeply into mass culture that you can hardly imagine what life looked like before *The Hobbit* and *The Lord of the Rings* trilogy became four of the most popular books of the twentieth century. Go into any bookstore; the extensive fantasy section you'll find there is a direct result of Tolkien's works having become a staple of early adolescence. So are the runic typefaces, the paperbacks festooned with magicians and omens of doom and the Welsh-sounding titles, all of which can be traced back in one way or another to Tolkien. His wizards and dwarfs and dark forces have as firm a grip on our imaginations as the stock characters of commedia dell'arte or vaudeville once did. The roles we play in Dungeons & Dragons are based on Tolkien heroes and villains. The Harry Potter juggernaut is inconceivable without Tolkien. J. K. Rowling's evil narcissist, Lord Voldemort, is a descendant of Tolkien's prideful Sauron; her uncanniest characters, the dementors—guards who terrorize prisoners by feeding off their happy thoughts, leaving them prey to their grimmest imaginings—are close cousins of Tolkien's Black Riders, ominous wraiths who prevail over their victims by inducing in them paralyzing fear.

Isn't influence like this a sign of greatness? T. A. Shippey thinks it is. Shippey is a Tolkienist who is also a professor of Old English philology and literature, and once taught at Oxford alongside Tolkien. In his book scheduled to be published in May 2001, *J.R.R. Tolkien: Author of the Century* (the subtitle is not ironic), Shippey offers up a bouquet of explanations for his subject's enduring popularity. They range from what you could call the theopolitical—that Tolkien's Christian-inspired views of good and evil are relevant to a world still reeling from Hitler and Stalin—to the allegorical, in which Frodo is featured as a savior not unlike Christ. Shippey's more persuasive argument, though, is philological. The reason Tolkien's work resonates so deeply, he says, is that it rings true to the ear of the English speaker.

Tolkien wasn't just a scholar of dead languages, he appears to have been possessed by them. When he was a student at Oxford, his hobby was creating new ones out of Gothic and Finnish grammar and roots (some of these authentic-sounding languages later appeared in his books). He did the same thing with the names of his characters, basing them on actual ancient English and Norse words. He viewed storytelling as a form of textual archaeology. His job as author was to resurrect names, personalities, events and, most of all, creatures—elves, dwarfs, dragons, goblins, orcs, Wargs—

buried deep within the strata of linguistic prehistory.

Take Wargs, preternaturally intelligent and malevolent wolves who live past the Edge of the Wild. Shippey believes Tolkien came up with them by reflecting on two words, the Old English "wearh," which means "outcast," and the Old Norse "vargr," which means both "wolf" and "outlaw." Vargr is a philological puzzle: Why would Old Norse have needed another word for "wolf" when it had the common word "ulfr"? Tolkien's creation implies an answer: There must have been an animal similar to a wolf, only outcast and evil.

Or Gandalf, the wizard who watches over hobbits and dwarfs like an anxious lesser deity. His name and those of most of the dwarfs in *The Hobbit* can be found in a section of an Old Norse poem that consists of a list of dwarfs' names; the passage is called "Dvergatal," or "Tally of the Dwarfs." Gandalf's name, though, is another philological problem. It contains the word "elf"—"alfr." But what's an elf doing in the "Tally of the Dwarfs," when ancient tradition made a clear distinction between the two creatures? Given that the first syllable of Gandalf could be interpreted as "wand," Shippey writes, Tolkien "seems to have concluded at some point that 'Gandalfr' meant 'staff-elf,' and that this must be a name for a wizard." Shippey speculates that Tolkien viewed the "Dvergatal" as "the last fading record of something that had once happened," and wrote *The Hobbit* as a gloss on that long-forgotten incident.

It is heady to know that a book you loved as a child conforms to such meticulous standards of mythical realism. Now I know why I felt that Tolkien ushered me into a world that had palpable existence, and why, when I visited Wales as a teenager, the street signs and village names felt so familiar. By basing Middle Earth on the shards of recovered languages and stories, he rooted it in something very like a collective preconscious. The question remains, however, whether this accomplishment is tantamount to literary greatness, as Shippey claims it is.

If you asked me, I'd say no. *The Hobbit*, which was written for children, came out almost twenty years before the trilogy. It's a light and charming book, and hobbits are refreshingly sane, middle-class creatures, especially compared with the powermongers and extremists they fall in among. But by the time you get to *The Fellowship of the Ring*, the first volume of *The Lord of the Rings*, Tolkien's tone has grown somber, even leaden. The villain of *The Hobbit* was a sarcastic and flirtatious dragon. The villain of *The Lord of the Rings* is absolute evil, which is distinctly less amusing. The farther into the trilogy you read, the less playful it gets. "There lie the woods of Lothlórien!" is the sort of thing characters say to one another a lot. To which the response is likely to be, "Let us hasten!"

The Lord of the Rings was written for adults, but unless you're a child it's difficult to accept its mounting portentousness without protest, as the price of entry into the longed-for past. One of the best things about growing up is realizing that grandeur doesn't have to be grandiose, nor does historical dialogue have to bristle with fusty archaisms. Tolkien dominates fantasy today because he gave his imaginings the aura of inevitability. But as a storyteller, he was betrayed by the very pedantry that made his creations memorable. He wandered over to the dark side, like an Elf-Lord gone bad. He formulated a high-minded belief in the importance of his mission as a literary preservationist, which turns out to be death to literature itself.

—*The New York Times Book Review,* April 22, 2001

DOES FRODO LIVE?

by Janet Adam Smith

F RODO LIVES!" The message is still printed on buttons, chalked up on subway platforms, though it is years since the first explosion of the campus cult. Does Tolkien live? Are his tales more endurable than the cult? Paul H. Kocher is sure that they are, and his *Master of Middle-earth: The Fiction of J.R.R. Tolkien* will help readers to see why; not readers who, like Edmund Wilson, are resistant to fairy tales and think them fit for children only, but those who, like Coleridge, believe that such tales can nourish imagination and extend human sympathies.

Mr. Kocher marks out the ground on which we should take Tolkien seriously. He is a sensible, unpedantic guide to Middle-earth; not for him the excessive symbol-hunting or structural analysis of some academic hobbit-fanciers. He points out patterns and correspondences that might be overlooked when the stories are gulped down at first reading. He discusses the ideas of morality and social order that underlie *The Lord of the Rings*, and the characteristics of the different kinds of beings (hobbits, elves, dwarves, etc.). He describes Tolkien's minor works, some hard to come by, and shows how they relate to the trilogy. He is sure that in telling his tales, Tolkien is telling us something about ourselves and our world that we ought to hear, and that this particular form was the right way to tell it. Fresh from the 279 pages of *The Hobbit* and the 1,069 of *The Lord of the Rings*, I agree with Mr. Kocher's general estimate, though here and there I have reservations.

The Hobbit, first published in 1937, was avowedly a children's book: the tale of Bilbo, who went on an adventure with dwarves and a wizard and came back with a ring and a load of treasure. (Hobbits are shown as pretty much like humans, but half the size, and nicer—keen on food and with deep, fruity laughs.) The tone of the story is confidential and friendly, very much like that of *The Wind in the Willows*: a grown-up unfolding marvels to a child, sometimes stopping to explain or comment ("It does not do to leave a live dragon out of your calculations"), often sharing a joke.

The prime joke of course is the contrast between commonsensical, home-loving hobbit Bilbo and the awful happenings he is involved in; some dread event is presented in high style—"with that the messengers departed swiftly"—to be instantly deflated: "Bilbo, of course, disapproved of the whole turn of affairs." When, almost accidentally, he picks up the magic ring in a dark and dangerous cavern, all he can think of is frying bacon and eggs in his own kitchen back home.

There are games with language, riddles and parodies. Bilbo on his dignity can sound like a pompous committeeman; Thorin, leader of the dwarves, like a patronizing company president handing out gold watches to staff with long service. The purpose of the quest for the dragon's hoard is outlined in a business letter ("Terms: cash on delivery, up to and not exceeding one fourteenth of total profits"). The sly monster Gollum talks to Bilbo in the false baby talk some adults think will ingratiate them with a child or animal: "What has it got in its pocketses?" The narrator nudges the child a little, so that he is sure to see the jokes.

Much is made of the comfort of the hobbits' home life: the cozy fireside, the lovely food—raspberry jam, apple tart, cold chicken, and pickles. The terrors of Mirkwood and the Misty Mountains are set off by the wholesome pleasures of the Shire. The tale begins with Bilbo smoking his pipe and ends with him reaching for his tobacco jar. Food and tobacco can be used and enjoyed; but owning things for owning's sake is the sickness of the dragon who sits on his mound of treasure. So Tolkien in his children's book introduces one of the main themes of his *Rings*.

Long meditated and worked over, *The Lord of the Rings* appeared in 1954 (Volume I) and 1955 (Volumes II and III). Tolkien was no longer talking especially to children, but he had taken a good deal over from his earlier tale. The reluctant hero is again a hobbit, Bilbo's heir, Frodo; but the world he is launched into is far more complex and mysterious. There is nothing in *The Hobbit* as frightening as the Black Riders who appear early in Frodo's quest, with their dead faces and wailings on the wind. With his companions—wizard, dwarf, elf, two men, and three other hobbits—Frodo encounters a greater variety of creatures and landscapes. Among the best new inventions are the Ents—tree-men fourteen feet high with deep, woodwind voices. (There is, by the way, a splendid photograph on the cover of Mr. Kocher's book of Tolkien asprawl among the gnarled and spreading roots of an antique tree, for all the world like Treebeard the Ent.)

Frodo's enemy is far worse than a dragon sitting on a pile of treasure; it is Evil itself. The Ring, which in *The Hobbit* was a stock fairy-tale property that could make its wearer invisible, has in *The Lord of the Rings* become a thing of vast and ambivalent power: catastrophic if it is allowed to fall into the hands of the Dark Lord Sauron, but corrupting if used by the good. Frodo's quest is to lose it in the fire in which it was forged on Mount Doom.

In this larger world of the *Rings*, possessiveness is the great evil: the wish to have power over others. The free people in the book "belong to themselves"—a phrase that often recurs. They do not wish for domination; they wish to use things properly, and not exploit them; when Gimli the dwarf speaks of the magical caverns of Helm's Deep and the beauty that could be made from their stone, he says, "We would tend these glades of flowering stone, not quarry them."

When *The Lord of the Rings* appeared in the mid-fifties, many readers took it as a parable of the awful power of the hydrogen bomb, which, like the Ring, corrupts its owners; one of Saruman's devilries is "a huge umbrella of cloud." Today, with Gimli's concern for the rocks, and the Ents' for the trees—the Dark Lord cuts down trees and does not care for growing things—one could as plausibly read it as a parable of the environment. Or—with Théoden's words to Saruman, "Were you ten times as wise you would have no right to rule me and mine for your own profit"—as a parable of anti-imperialism.

That it can offer such different interpretations is one of the strengths of the saga. Tolkien's Sauron and Saruman and Gollum embody perennial forces of greed, cruelty, and aggression; readers will tend to pick out the manifestations of these forces which are most in their own minds.

The moral world is not black and white. The questers can be tempted and fall, the evil Gollum can at the climax be an instrument for good. But none of this would count if Tolkien were not also a superb storyteller: keeping the reader in cliff-hanging suspense, rewarding him with a rescue, a victory, or a homecoming; now displaying armies and battles, now following a solitary hero. His world fits together as with Stevenson's *Treasure Island*, one suspects that the maps came first. (A complaint about the paperback edition is that the maps are too small, and you are deprived of the pleasure of following the journeys in detail.)

Whatever his metaphysical preoccupations, Tolkien's physical perceptions are acute: the cliffs Frodo climbs, the thorny brakes he battles through, are almost painfully real to our imaginations. Tolkien believes in his world, and convinces us that there is far more of it than has found its way into his books. He is not stretching his invention: he is writing from abundance.

He is of course writing with an army of allies behind him, from the anonymous makers of the sagas and *Beowulf* and the *Battle of Maldon* to Macauley and William Morris. These, with Malory and Spenser and countless others, have been his familiars and he has taken from them as he needed. Spotting "sources" and tracking echoes will not add to the value of reading *The Lord of the Rings*, but it can give an extra pleasure: the saga becomes a journey through the literature of Western Europe (sometimes it seems like a journey through the Oxford English School) as well as a journey through Middle-earth to Mount Doom.

When the men of Rohan muster, it is to an Anglo-Saxon (or early Auden) beat:

> *From dark Dunharrow in the dim morning*
> *with thane and captain rode Thengel's son:*
> *to Edoras he came, the ancient halls*
> *of the Mark-wardens mist-enshrouded; . . .*

When Frodo's strength ebbs under the Barrow-wight and he thinks he has come to the terrible end of his adventure, "The thought hardened him" like the warrior at the Battle of Maldon whose word when the shield-wall broke was:

> *The will shall be harder,*
> *the courage shall be keener,*
> *Spirit shall grow great,*
> *as our strength falls away.*

When the swords flash, Gúthwine and Andúri, we are with the *Chanson de Roland*; when dead warriors float out on a barge to sea, with Malory (and is not Mordor, the country of the Dark Lord, linked with Malory's Mordred, King Arthur's betrayer?). The beauty of the restored city Minas Tirith—"It was filled with trees and with fountains, and its gates were wrought of mithril and steel, and its streets were paved with white marble"—recalls the medieval hymns about Jerusalem; the timeless enchantment of the land of Lórien, or the spring valleys of Ithilien, make one think of paradise gardens from the book of Genesis to William Morris. The dying land that Frodo passes through on the last stage of his journey might be the waste traversed by Browning's Childe Roland on the way to *his* Dark Tower.

There are less lofty echoes. Early in the saga there is a chapter called "At the Sign of the Prancing Pony" which, with a jolly innkeeper, a dark stranger in the corner, sinister wayfarers peering round doors, is in the key of Stevenson's *St. Ives* or Buchan's *Midwinter* or many another historical romance with mysterious encounters at lonely crossroads inns.

About this last mode, I feel an uneasiness that extends to much of the hobbit element in *The Lord of the Rings*. The device of the hobbits—small people, peaceful, merry, unheroic, who can't live long on the heights—is excellent. They stand for stability and common sense, as necessary to life as enterprise and discovery. The happy humdrum life of the hobbits in their Shire is a necessary counterpart to the magical and heroic happenings in the kingdom of Rohan and Gondor. But to my mind Tolkien's imagination fed on thinner stuff when he created the world beyond its borders.

Behind that world is epic and saga, legend and fairy tale; behind the Shire is a sort of Chestertonian myth of Merrie England, a much thinner affair. With their tobacco and ale, their platters and leather jerkins, their wholesome tastes and deep, fruity laughs, their pipe-smoking male coziness, and jolly-good-fellowship, hobbits can be as phony as a Christmas card with stagecoaches and lighted inns.

Auden, reviewing *The Fellowship of the Ring*, observed that in their thinking and sensibility, hobbits "closely resemble those arcadian villagers who so frequently populate British detective stories." He is quite right: particularly when they talk. Far the worst is Sam Gamgee, Frodo's servant. Here he is addressing the wizard:

"Lor bless you, Mr. Gandalf, sir! Nothing! Leastways I was just trimming the grass-border under the window, if you follow me."

Here describing the lady of Lórien:

"You should see her, indeed you should, sir. I am only a hobbit and gardening's my job at home, sir, if you understand me, and I'm not much good at poetry—not at making it: a bit of a comic rhyme perhaps now and again. . . ."

"Mr. Frodo, sir," is Sam's address to his master at even the most desperate moments of their adventure together. It is grating.

Yet—even with wrong notes like this—Tolkien's own beneficent ring of power is that he is a master of language. As the quotations will have shown, he can command a host of styles, though not all with equal ease. He suits the language to the scene—tough Anglo-Saxon and saga words and rhythms for battles and forays, softer romantic ones for enchanted Lórien and Rivendell. He cherishes words that have fallen out of use, and he brings stale figures of speech to life: as Frodo comes to the chasm on Mount Doom where he is to throw the ring on the fire—and for an instant hesitates—suddenly we realize he is standing at the Crack of Doom. Tolkien invents, brilliantly, "good" language—

> *A Elbereth Gilthoniel*
> *o menel palan-diriel.* . . .

and "bad"—"*Ash nazg durbatuluk, ash nazg gimbatul, ash nazg thrakatuluk agh burzum-ishi krimpatul.*" (The prevalence of *k* and *l* in the "bad" language made me wonder if these are always evil combinations—such as Ku Klux Klan—but then I though of Tolkien, and ceased speculating.)

Tolkien's attitude to language is part of his attitude to history (here, if we like, we can find parallels with Eliot and Pound and David Jones of *The Anathemata*): to recapture and re-animate the words of the past is to recapture something of ourselves; for we carry the past in us, and our existence, like Frodo's quest, is only an episode in an age-long and continuing drama.

To name things rightly is to have strength: the evil Lieutenant of the Dark Tower has forgotten his own name. Words are power, so evil turns them upside down. When Saruman, trapped in his stronghold of Orthanc, speaks seemingly gentle and reasonable words, the hobbits and men are half persuaded; but Gimli the dwarf spots the falseness of tone as sharply as if he had been to school with a New Critic: "The words of this wizard stand on their heads.... In the language of Orthanc help means ruin, and saving means slaying. ..."

In days like ours when help can still mean ruin and saving mean slaying, when evil and horrible acts can be given wrong names—"redevelopment" for people losing their homes, "defoliation" for forests and fields blasted with poison—a book which sharpens a sense of words, their power and proper meaning, is to be praised. For all the excesses of the Tolkien cult, there could be many a worse one.

—*The New York Review of Books*, December 14, 1972

LORD OF THE GEEKS

by Julian Dibbell

In 1961, five years after publication of the final volume in John Ronald Reuel Tolkien's three-part fantasy epic, *The Lord of the Rings*, the formidable English literary critic Philip Toynbee announced with great relief that popular enthusiasm for Tolkien was now thoroughly tapped out and his works were finally on their way to "merciful oblivion." Nice call, Phil: Four years later, the first American paperback edition of *The Lord of the Rings* appeared, and the modestly best-selling book—the tale of brave little hobbit Frodo Baggins's quest to destroy the Ring of Power and save Middle Earth from the Dark Lord Sauron—blew up to a youth-cultural legend. Three million copies were sold between 1965 and 1968; the curly-haired Frodo and his white-bearded wizardly protector Gandalf became hippie icons; and merry pranksters decked the walls of college campuses with such graffiti as "J.R.R. Tolkien is hobbit forming" and "Frodo Lives."

He still does, in case you hadn't noticed. Even as you read this, the living face of Frodo Baggins is probably shining, ten feet tall, on a movie screen near you, embodied by teen actor Elijah Wood in a trailer for New Line Cinema's upcoming *Fellowship of the Ring*, the first installment in a slavishly faithful three-film rendering of the *Ring* trilogy. When the movie opens in December, it will land like a mothership in the midst of a global fandom that has by now swelled the sales figure for

Tolkien's masterwork to over fifty million copies (not counting the forty million sales of its 1938 predecessor, *The Hobbit*).
The Tolkienite hordes have been flooding Web sites for
months with gossip and debate about the film. Add in every
online discussion about the genealogy of the kings of Gondor,
every argument over the syntax of the Elven Quenya dialect,
and the monthly textual output of the world's Tolkien-
flavored chat rooms and message boards probably exceeds,
kilobyte for kilobyte, the 1400 pages of *The Lord of the Rings*
itself. In short, the year 2001 finds Tolkien's following bigger
and busier than at any other period in the four decades since
Philip Toynbee wrote its obituary.

What that amounts to in the greater pop cultural scheme
of things, of course, is harder to say than it used to be. Back in
the days when Tolkien was still alive and in the habit of refer-
ring to his shaggy, puff-sleeved fans as "my deplorable cultus"
(he was a straitlaced, archconservative Catholic himself), they
were easily mistaken for flower children, or at least fellow trav-
elers on the road to a global transformation of consciousness
through drugs, electrified music, and other forms of postin-
dustrial enchantment. But now that the world-historical
context has simmered down and a somewhat tamer generation has filled out the hobbit-loving ranks, everyone can see
they're just geeks.

Or something even geekier, arguably: ur-geeks. Keepers of
the geek flame. For if *The Lord of the Rings* is not the sine qua
non of geek culture, it's hard to think what is. After all, the
vast genre of fantasy fiction is, along with sci-fi, one of the two
great narrative flows feeding the Nerd Nation's imaginative
life, and nobody doubts that Tolkien single-handedly invented it. And that's not even counting the immense subcultural
continent that is Dungeons & Dragons and every role-playing
game descended from it—from the complex, online time-
suck EverQuest to the Japanimated children's saga
DragonBallZ—all of which testify to the formative influence
of the Tolkien mythos. Throw in *Star Wars* (as Tolkienesque a

space opera as ever there was) and the argument is pretty much a lock: Without the lucidly imagined geography of Middle Earth and the archetypal characters Tolkien stocked it with—the grave wizards, stout dwarves, evil orcs, and above all, plucky, permanently adolescent hobbits—geekdom as we know it would simply not exist.

If you feel that's no particularly meaningful achievement, I understand. But maybe you could indulge me and imagine, just for a moment, that the fact that we live in a world increasingly made by geeks actually makes their collective imagination worth understanding. Think about computers, their evolution shaped by a hacker culture that insisted some of the earliest dot-matrix printers be programmed to produce the elvish Fëanorian script. Think about the Internet, whose founding architects included the D&D fanatic who created the Adventure, the very first, very Tolkienized online role-playing game. Think, for a moment, about these profoundly transformative technologies. And then consider the possibility that the structures of feeling we inherit from them might just have some intimate connection to the dream life of the people who designed them. Consider, in other words, the possibility that *The Lord of the Rings*, geek culture's defining literary creation, might just be one of the defining literary creations of our age.

That *The Lord of the Rings* belongs among the most important works of modern Western literature is not an unheard-of notion, but it's not exactly a blue-ribbon one either, True, in some of the first reviews of the trilogy, Tolkien's best friend, C. S. Lewis, did call it a groundbreaking successor to the *Odyssey*, and W. H. Auden reckoned it was right up there with Milton's *Paradise Lost*. But when übercritic Edmund Wilson published a bruising smackdown in *The Nation* ("Oo, Those Awful Orcs," April 14, 1956) dismissing the book as "balderdash" and "juvenile trash," he sent Tolkien's critical stock into a long, steady tailspin from which it has yet to recover. By late 1996, when a survey of British readers crowned *The Lord of the*

Rings "the greatest book of the twentieth century," the dismay that set in among Britain's credentialed literati was as predictable as it was over-the-top. Germaine Greer, who arrived at Cambridge as a student in 1964, wrote "it has been my nightmare that Tolkien would turn out to be the most influential writer of the twentieth century. The bad dream has materialised." Nor does the official stance seem to have softened any since. Just a few weeks ago critic Judith Shulevitz went to the trouble of reminding us all, in the pages of *The New York Times Book Review*, that no modern work of fiction in which people say things like "There lie the woods of Lothlórien! . . . Let us hasten!" can be anything less than "death to literature itself."

Shulevitz made these remarks in response to claims very much to the contrary, advanced in T. Shippey's new critical assessment, *J.R.R.Tolkien: Author of the Century*, published by Houghton Mifflin last month. Shippey is a professor of Old English, just as Tolkien was—Shippey even shared teaching duties with Tolkien at Oxford for a brief time—and he seems to take just a tad personally the general critical disdain heaped upon his former colleague. But while his indignation gets a little out of hand, his argument is a sober one, aimed at setting Tolkien alongside such epic poets of the twentieth-century condition as Orwell, Joyce, and Pynchon. *The Lord of the Rings*, he insists, constitutes "a deeply serious response to what will be seen in the end as the major issues of his century: the origin and nature of evil . . . ; human existence . . . without the support of divine revelation; cultural relativity; and the corruptions and continuities of language." But in fact, deeply serious or not, Tolkien's actual responses to these issues are so deeply unengaged with the twentieth century cultural mainstream as to seem willfully out of it.

A lovely list of issues indeed. The problem, though, is that, deeply serious or not, Tolkien's responses to them were those of a man whose head resided in the twentieth century but whose heart just wasn't in it. He was a medievalist in more ways than one, and to read his work as Shippey proposes, with the concerns of modernist literature in mind, is to invite the sort of exasperation you might feel if you were in the mood for *Madame Bovary* and got handed *Beowulf* instead. Tolkien's theory of evil? Well, orcs are, our heroes aren't, and that about sums it up. Tolkien's take on "human existence"? A hard gig, certainly, full of danger and touch decisions, but fortunately not enough to threaten the wise Gandalf, the noble Aragorn, the sly Saruman, or any of Tolkien's other characters with more than the occasional moment of psychological complexity. And as for "cultural relativity," hoo boy. By the time you have read your third or fourth description of the orcs as "swarthy" and "slant-eyed" you will either have checked your late-modern political sensitivities at the door or thrown the book at the wall.

But ultimately, the real problem with Shippey's approach is the same one that dogs almost all attempts to wring serious literary meaning out of *The Lord of the Rings*: It fails to take Tolkien's literary project as seriously as he took it himself. "I cordially dislike allegory in all its manifestations," he famously wrote in one foreword to the trilogy, warning readers against the temptation of finding in it "any inner meaning or 'message.'" Nearly every thoughtful piece of Tolkien criticism makes some kind of nod to the letter of that admonition, but very few can resist violating its spirit. For some, the "inner meaning" of *The Lord of the Rings* has been a bluntly topical allegory of, say, World War II or eco-activism (Sauron is Hitler and the Ring is the atomic bomb; Sauron is the enemy of Gaia and the Ring is industrial technology). For more high-minded exegetes, like Auden and Shippey, the meanings are more abstract (Frodo's quest is the Quest of Everyman to come to know himself; Frodo's struggle with the Ring's corrupting influence is society's struggle with the burden of power). But either way, these critics' sense of the worthiness of the trilogy compels them to sniff out its significance, often as not at the expense of any true grasp of what Tolkien's point and power really are.

So what is his point then? What is his power? Strip away his meaning and what is left? Well, Middle-earth itself. Or rather his invention of it—a powerful, lifelong act that produced at least twelve volumes of background notes on the history and languages of that imaginary world. Some might call this make-believe, others might call it simulation, still others would call it hallucination. All three explain why, as an unnamed British smartass observed in a 1992 edition of *Private Eye,* Tolkien's writing appeals less to critics than "to those with the mental age of a child, computer programmers, hippies and most Americans." There is in America—and anywhere else the engines of postmodernity run at full tilt—a growing cultural fascination with the elasticity of reality, and with it a growing urge to tinker at reality's stretchiest edges. Literature, as the critics now understand it, doesn't satisfy this urge. But child's play has always done the trick. Psychedelics too. And now, more and more, our technologies are at it as well. Already, deep, complex computer games like the Sims and Black and White anticipate an era when critics locate culture's center of gravity not in books but in elaborate digital simulations. And when they do, a few may recall that it was Tolkien, lord of the greeks, who announced the shift.

—*The Village Voice,* June 6, 2001

The Reader

THE LORD OF THE RINGS

Discussion Questions

* The Fellowship of the Ring *

1. "I am in fact a *Hobbit* (in all but size)," wrote Tolkien to a correspondent in 1958. "I like gardens, trees and unmechanized farmlands; I smoke a pipe, and like good plain food (unrefrigerated) ... like, and even dare to wear these dull days, ornamental waistcoats. I am fond of mushrooms (out of a field); have a very simple sense of humour (which even my appreciative critics find tiresome); I go to bed late and get up late (when possible). I do not travel much." How would you describe the hobbits' way of life and behavior? How are they different from us, and how are they similar?

2. "I have, I suppose," wrote Tolkien in 1958, "constructed an imaginary *time*, but kept my feet on my own mother-earth for *place*. ... *Middle-earth* is ... a modernization or alteration ... of an old word for the inhabited world of Men." How has Tolkien created a sense of an actual world with seemingly real landmarks and a credible imaginary history?

3. How is it significant that Gollum had been a hobbit before acquiring the Ring? To what degree can the Ring's powers be used for good or evil depending on the moral character of its bearer?

4. How would you explain Sam Gamgee's determination to stay with Frodo no matter what? What qualities, talents, and shortcomings does Sam reveal as the journey continues, and how is he changed by his experiences?

5. How do the Black Riders' methods of sensing their surroundings link them with evil and the dark and make them particularly terrifying? What do you think Strider means when, speaking of the Dark Riders, he tells the hobbits, "You fear them but you do not fear them enough, yet" (p. 177)?

6. After being wounded in his fight with the Black Rider, Frodo realizes "that in putting on the Ring he obeyed not his own desire but the commanding wish of his enemies" (p. 211)? In what other instances do characters act against their own best interests, and why?

7. "And he that breaks a thing to find out what it is has left the path of wisdom," Gandalf proclaims to Saruman (p. 272). What instances do you find—in *The Lord of the Rings* and your own world—of attempts to break things in order to find out what they are or how they work?

8. Saruman advises Gandalf that their best choice would be to join with the "new Power" that is rising so "to direct its course, to control it" (p. 272). To what extent is the main theme of *The Lord of the Rings* the uses, abuses, and consequences of power?

9. Why does Gandalf say that it would "be well to trust rather in friendship than to great wisdom" in deciding who should accompany Frodo (p. 289)? In what ways might friendship be more powerful than great wisdom?

10. Boromir argues that the Company's choice is between destroying the Ring and destroying "the armed might of the

Dark Lord" (p. 385). Is his argument valid? To what extent does the completion of either task depend upon the completion of the other?

✷ The Two Towers ✷

1. "Do we walk in legends or on the green earth in the daylight?" Éomer asks. How would you explain Aragorn's response: "A man may do both" (p. 37)?

2. Merry and Pippin look back out of the shadows of Fangorn, "little furtive figures that in the dim light looked like elf-children in the deeps of time peering out of the Wild Wood in wonder at their First Dawn" (p. 62). How do the initial innocence and lasting hopefulness of the hobbits provide a balance to the more complex experience of men, the Elves' ancient knowledge, Gandalf's wisdom, and Sauron's evil?

3. Treebeard says of Saruman, "He has a mind of metal and wheels; and he does not care for growing things" (p. 76). How does Tolkien illustrate the limitations and menace of technology and the benevolence and rewards of growing things?

4. "Good and ill have not changed since yesteryear," says Aragorn, "nor are they one thing among Elves and Dwarves and another among Men" (p. 41). Why does the struggle between good and evil continue much the same from age to age, from place to place, and from one group to another?

5. If a wizard as wise and powerful as Saruman can be corrupted, what chance does anyone have against the forces of evil? How are Gandalf, Aragorn, Frodo, and others able to withstand the temptations and desires to which Saruman, Gollum, Wormtongue, and others succumb?

6. "Often does hatred hurt itself," says Gandalf (p. 190). How might this be true of hatred and evil in the novel and in life?

7. What lineage does Faramir claim, and how is it related to Aragorn's? What other family pedigrees does Tolkien present, and why do you think family histories and ancestral lines are so important?

8. When Sam speaks about "the old tales and songs," what does he say characterizes the tales and songs that really matter? How does he distinguish between "the best tales to hear" and "the best tales to get landed in" (pp. 320-21)?

9. What do you find characteristic of each dwelling and community in the various regions of Middle-earth? How is each specific in terms of its locale and the culture of its residents?

10. In what ways are Faramir and Gandalf alike? How is Sam's observation that Faramir reminds him of Gandalf supported by Faramir's actions and statements?

* The Return of the King *

1. How are Gandalf's power, wisdom, and majesty manifested throughout the novel? How, and with what consequences, does he apply his powers in his relationships with the various other residents of Middle-earth?

2. How would you characterize the relationship between Faramir and his father, Denethor? What causes Denethor to be so critical of his son?

3. Éowyn protests to Aragorn, "All your words are but to say:

you are a woman, and your part is in the house" (p. 58). What are Éowyn's and Aragorn's opposing views of a woman's duties and roles?

4. How would you describe "the joy of battle" that comes upon the Rohirrim as they advance on besieged Minas Tirith (p. 113)? What other instances of it occur in the novel? What might be the consequences of giving oneself up to "the joy of battle"?

5. Mourning Théoden in the Houses of Healing, Merry apologizes for his sarcasm by saying, "But it is the way of my people to use light words at such times and say less than they mean. We fear to say too much. It robs us of the right words when a jest is out of place" (p. 146). What does he mean? At what other serious moments do the hobbits engage in humor?

6. "It is best to love first what you are fitted to love, I suppose," says Merry; "you must start somewhere and have some roots" (p. 146). How is this true of the hobbits and others?

7. When Sam sees the white star twinkling through the cloud-wrack above the Morgai, "the beauty of it smote his heart [and] the thought pierced him that in the end the Shadow was only a small and passing thing" (p. 199). In what ways is the Shadow of evil finally only "a small and passing thing"?

8. What does Gandalf mean when he tells the hobbits that they must settle the affairs of the Shire themselves? In what ways have they been "trained" for just that task, according to Gandalf, and in what ways have they "grown indeed very high" (p. 275)?

9. Just before Frodo boards the ship in the Grey Havens, he says to Sam, "It must often be so, Sam, when things are in

danger: some one has to give them up, lose them, so that others may keep them" (p. 309). How is this true in the novel and in our own lives?

10. What kind of lives do you think Sam and Rosie, Merry, and Pippin have after Frodo and Gandalf's departure? What might be the significance of the novel ending with Sam and Rosie enjoying the comfort and love of their new home (p. 311)?

Tolkien of Affection: Two Puzzles
by Mel Rosen

Across

1 Luzon volcano
5 Familiar initials in math
8 Hindu gentleman
12 ____ on (urges)
16 Following
18 River to the Caspian
20 Zeal
21 Nov. 1957 space traveler
23 Who
27 Moroccan port
28 Word with welcome or place
29 Part of many German names
30 Fell for
31 Indian groom: Var.
32 Public warehouses
35 Usual food and drink
37 Three ____ match
38 What
43 Westphalian city
44 Former French coin
45 Youngster
46 Canape cover
49 Ruth's mother-in-law
52 Ingredient for 24 Down
56 When
63 Berne's river
64 Provokes sarcastically
65 Name in Dublin
66 Wax: comb. form
67 Gumshoes
68 Building extension
69 Caesar's greeting
70 Southeast Asian
71 Wages or reward. In N.Z.
72 English country festivals
74 Looking up
77 Worthless quantity of beans
78 Where
83 Old dirks
84 Competitor
85 Service ending
86 Air: Comb. form
88 Immobilize, in wrestling
89 Shock
93 Why
101 Watergate figure
102 Central point
103 Worshipful one
104 Cross
106 Tint
107 Word with up or off
108 Spinks's predecessor
109 A word considered only as letters or sounds
111 How
117 Luxury cut
118 Derby hopeful
119 New Haven draw
120 Kind of rocket
121 Coat-of-arms feature
122 Living-room item
123 A thing, in law
124 Org.

Down

1 William Howard and Robert A.
2 Nervous
3 "Right now!"
4 Sherpa perches
5 Books composed of sheets folded twice
6 Energy unit
7 Memorable U.N. name
8 Worst
9 Occurring by turns: Abbr.
10 Scrooge word
11 Rough
12 N.C. college
13 Salesman's gift
14 Asian ape
15 Enjoying the slopes
17 Louis Philippe, e.g.
19 Sweetened the soil
22 " ____ boy!"
24 Pilsener and lager
25 Boss Tweed's nemesis
26 Stopover
33 Certain vote
34 Medieval banner
35 Conclude
36 Chit
39 __ off (irate)
40 Half: Prefix
41 Comedienne Martha
42 Concept
46 Light carriage
47 Age tobacco
48 Very, to Pierre
50 Astern
51 Meditation syllables
53 File in a certain repository
54 Sneak home late
55 Excite
56 "Paper Moon" star and others
57 On ____ (carousing)
58 Italian rooster
59 Swiss mathematician of the 1700s
60 Sap
61 Resided
62 Cold month in Madrid
70 Sci-fi movie of the 50's
73 Discord
74 Gun a motor
75 Wave, in Malaga
76 River of Argentina
79 Unhearing
80 Bone: Comb. form
81 Clue
82 What pride precedeth
87 " ____ La Mancha"
88 Pea package
90 72 for 18, usually
91 Glimpses of coming attractions: Var.
92 Tire city
93 Golden-rule words
94 Devonshire city
95 Subjects of conversation
96 Aura
97 Improve morally
98 Nagyvarad, to a Rumanian
99 Capek creations
100 Poetic sorrows
101 Letters from Greece
105 Exorcist's target
107 Lap dog, for short
108 Nick and Nora's dog
110 Lineman: Abbr.
112 "2001" feature
113 Milne creature
114 Sprite
115 Impair
116 Corrida cry

Directions:

An acrostic puzzle is not difficult to solve. If you can correctly guess as many as four or five WORDS, you have made a good start.

Each numbered blank represents one letter in the WORD to be defined. Answer as many WORDS as you can. Then copy the letters in each WORD to their corresponding numbered spaces in the diagram.

When completed, the diagram reads across only, showing a passage from a Tolkien book. The black squares indicate where a word ends and another begins. Words carry over to the next line if there is no black square at the end of a line.

You should discover words and phrases forming in the diagram as letters are filled in. Work backwards from the diagram to the WORDS, and in that way, guess still more WORDS. The letters in the upper right-hand corner of the squares in the diagram show the WORD from which a particular square's letter comes. The first letter of each WORD, in order, spells the complete name of the book from which the passage is taken.

1 B	2 N	■	3 X	4 J	5 L	■	6 C	7 B	8 N	9 H	10 Z	11 A	■	12 A	13 L	
14 Z	15 C	16 F	17 J	■	18 M	19 W	■	20 G	21 U	22 K	23 Q	24 Z	25 A	26 R	27 L	
28 L	29 P	30 V	31 G	32 Z	33 A	■	34 W	35 F	36 C	■	37 E	38 N	39 L	■	40 G	41 L
42 Y	■	43 O	44 E	45 F	46 R	47 N	■	48 I	49 X	50 B	51 S	■	52 N	53 E	54 Z	55 J
■	56 B	57 Y	■	58 A	59 W	60 Q	■	61 U	62 M	63 H	64 J	■	65 T	66 A	67 V	68 J
■	69 V	70 G	■	71 M	72 Y	73 B	■	74 B	■	75 E	76 Z	77 I	78 P	79 J	80 T	
81 Z	82 C	83 U	84 K	■	85 Z	86 E	87 O	■	88 L	89 V	■	90 L	91 N	92 M	93 Z	94 E
■	95 I	96 T	97 W	98 V	99 C	■	100 K	101 A	102 Z	103 Q	104 O	■	105 Z	106 A	107 O	108 Q
109 L	110 F	111 Z	■	112 Q	113 Z	■	114 U	115 L	116 K	■	117 V	118 M	119 X	120 D	■	121 N
122 V	123 F	■	124 O	125 F	126 W	127 R	■	128 J	129 V	■	130 G	131 S	132 Z	■	133 M	134 Z
135 S	136 F	■	137 Z	138 Q	139 I	■	140 J	141 N	142 Z	143 D	■	144 H	145 W	146 N	■	147 D
148 Q	149 Z	150 K	151 O	152 B	■	153 P	154 E	155 Z	156 H	■	157 V	158 I	■	159 I	160 X	161 L
162 E	163 W	164 C	165 Y	■	166 K	167 V	■	168 L	169 Z	170 N	171 J	■	172 F	173 Y	174 Q	175 N
176 P	■	177 Y	178 O	179 D	180 R	■	181 G	182 L	183 Q	184 U	185 Y	186 N	187 O	188 A	■	189 E
190 Z	191 J	192 L	■	193 V	194 D	195 P	■	196 C	197 P	198 Z	199 T	■	200 F	201 K	202 Z	
203 D	204 U	205 O	206 Z	207 F	■	208 D	■	209 A	210 U	211 L	212 D	213 Z	214 G	■	215 E	216 Z
217 S	■	218 N	219 H	■	220 E	221 Q	222 W	223 K	■	224 Z	225 J	226 A	■	227 C	228 X	

DEFINITIONS

WORDS

A. See Word Y.

— — — — — — — — — — —
33 58 66 101 11 12 226 106 209 188 25

B. Commemorative occasion

— — — — — — —
1 7 50 56 73 74 152

C. Town on Long Lake, below the Lonely Mountain

— — — — — — — —
164 196 6 15 36 82 99 227

D. Came to pass

— — — — — — — —
194 208 212 143 120 203 179 147

E. Insulting name for a spider (2 words)

— — — — — — — — — — —
189 75 215 37 154 220 86 44 162 94 53

F. Old Took's great-granduncle

— — — — — — — — — —
200 45 172 110 123 35 125 207 136 16

G. Moistened

— — — — — — —
40 31 181 214 130 70 20

H. Feasting and total comfort, to Bilbo Baggins

— — — — —
63 156 219 144 9

I. Added a spigot, to a cider barrel perhaps

— — — — — —
77 95 159 48 158 139

J. Thorin's last name

— — — — — — — — — — —
225 4 17 191 64 55 171 128 68 79 140

K. Paid back: took vengeance

— — — — — — — —
22 116 100 201 166 84 223 150

L. " _ , the spear is long, the arrow swift, the Gate is strong" (4 words from a song of the dwarves)

— — — — — — — —
109 115 28 27 168 39 90 161

— — — — — — —
41 5 13 88 182 192 211

M. Sound of laughter

— — — — — —
71 18 92 62 118 133

N. Line of demarcation near the Misty Mountains (4 words)

— — — — — — — — — — — — —
2 47 175 52 91 121 170 218 141 38 186 8 146

DEFINITIONS   WORDS

O. Elrond's Last
Homely House

__ __ __ __ __ __ __ __ __
43 107 205 178 187 87 104 151 124

P. Stimulate

__ __ __ __ __ __
176 29 153 197 78 195

Q. The Heart of the
Mountain, buried
with Thorin

__ __ __ __ __ __ __ __ __ __
221 174 23 108 183 60 103 112 138 148

R. The Shire, to Bilbo:
The Lonely
Mountain, to Smaug

__ __ __ __
46 127 26 180

S. Smaug, after the
black arrow

__ __ __ __
135 51 131 217

T. Complain

__ __ __ __
96 199 80 65

U. Stir up

__ __ __ __ __ __ __
83 184 210 61 21 114 204

V. "__ and tread on the fat!
Pour the milk on the
pantry floor!" (3 words
from another song)

__ __ __ __ __ __ __ __ __ __ __
30 98 129 193 69 89 67 117 122 167 157

W. "Elves and Men! To
Me! O my __ " (rally-
ing cry during the
Battle of Five Armies)

__ __ __ __ __ __ __ __
222 59 145 19 34 97 163 126

X. Watchful: observant

__ __ __ __ __
160 3 49 119 228

Y. The wandering wizard

__ __ __ __ __ __ __
42 72 57 165 173 185 177

Z. Relative of water skis

__ __ __ __ __ __ __ __ __
137 105 10 85 32 213 149 224 54

Ẓ. Quality imparted by a
ring

__ __ __ __ __ __ __ __ __ __ __ __
102 24 190 216 132 134 81 76 155 169 202 111

Ẕ. In demand: craved

__ __ __ __ __ __
113 93 142 14 206 198

Solutions to Puzzles

THE HOBBIT: OR THERE AND BACK AGAIN: He was Gollum—as dark as darkness, except for two big round pale eyes in his thin face. He had a little boat, and he rowed about quite quietly on the lake; for lake it was, wide and deep and deadly cold. He paddled it with large feet dangling over the side, but never a ripple did he make. Not he.

WORDS:

A. Thaumaturge	H. Ideal	O. Rivendell	V. Cut the cloth
B. Holiday	I. Tapped	P. Excite	W. Kinsfolk
C. Esgaroth	J. Oakenshield	Q. Arkenstone	X. Awake
D. Happened	K. Requited	R. Nest	Y. Gandalf
E. Old Tomnoddy	L. The sword is sharp	S. Dead	Z. Aquaplane
F Bullroarer	M. Hawhaw	T. Beef	Z1. Invisibility
G. Bedewed	N. Edge of the wild	U. Agitate	Z2. Needed

THE MIDDLE-EARTH GOURMET

by Maureen Bayha and Alida Becker

There's almost nothing a hobbit loves quite so much as a good meal—unless it's an unexpected, extra meal. Civilized life in the Shire revolves around "plenty of food at regular and frequent intervals," and the pantries of hobbit *smials* are stocked with enough delicacies so that no opportunity for feasting needs to be missed. A hobbit larder can produce, on a moment's notice, the makings of a high tea or a family picnic, or even provisions for a journey to Erebor.

Proper hobbit food is rather simple and hearty, much like English country fare. Although the dish hobbits talk of most often is a simple breakfast of fried eggs and bacon, they're certainly not willing to slight the other meals on their daily schedule. Any time of day, hobbits are always interested in "something hot out of the pot," and if that something is liberally laced with mushrooms, so much the better.

In fairness, though, we must remember that other denizens of Middle-earth have to get by with a bite now and then, so our collection of recipes includes a bit of "fissh" for Gollum, a leg of mutton for a troll, and seedcake for the dwarves. Alas, the food of the elves cannot be duplicated by other Middle-earth cooks; and as for that of the orcs, who'd want to?

Frodo's Scones

In a large bowl, sift together 2 cups of sifted all-purpose flour, 1/2 teaspoon of salt, 1/2 teaspoon of baking powder, and 1 tablespoon of sugar. Cut in 1/2 cup of shortening. Add 1 cup of raisins or currants. Make a well and add enough buttermilk to form a stiff dough. Roll out 1/4 to 1/2 inch thick on a floured board. Fry on a lightly greased griddle for 7 to 10 minutes. Turn. Fry for 7 to 10 minutes more and serve.

Bilbo's Orange Marmalade

Wash, dry, and peel 2 pounds of smooth, unblemished oranges. Cover the peel with cold water and simmer for 2 hours, until it is tender. Slice the oranges very thin and mix with 2 pounds of sugar. Drain the peel, cool, and scrape out the white pith. Slice the peel very thin. Combine the oranges and peel, and stir well. Simmer over a low heat until thick. Pour into hot, sterilized jars and cover.

Smaug's Gems

Combine 1 cup of vanilla wafer crumbs, 1 cup of confectioners' sugar, 1 cup of chopped nuts, and 1 tablespoon of cocoa. Add 2 tablespoons of light corn syrup and 1/4 cup of whisky. Mix well and shape into 1 inch balls. Roll in confectioners' sugar and place in an air-tight container. Store in the refrigerator.

Fruit Fool à la Sackville-Baggins

Cook a quart of berries (gooseberries, raspberries, or blackberries) in a heavy saucepan over a low heat for 30 minutes, stirring and mashing constantly. Add 1 cup of sugar and simmer until the sugar is dissolved. Purée in a fine sieve, cover, and refrigerate. Just before serving, whip 3 cups of heavy cream and fold it into the fruit mixture. Serve at once.

Merry's Mulled Cider

Mix together 2 quarts of apple cider, 20 whole cloves, 1/2 cup of sugar, 12 sticks of cinnamon, 14 whole allspice, and 1/2 teaspoon of salt. Bring to a boil. Simmer for 15 minutes. Keep warm. Strain and serve in a mug with a lemon slice.

Mrs. Maggot's Cottage Pie

Slice a large onion and 2 carrots and sauté in bacon fat until the onions are limp. Add 1 pound of cubed beef, 1 tablespoon of flour, and salt and pepper to taste. Sauté for several minutes, then add 1/2 cup of beef stock and simmer for 20 to 30 minutes. Peel and quarter 1 pound of potatoes and boil until soft. Mash with 2 to 3 tablespoons of butter and enough milk to make a soft mash. Season with salt and pepper. Put the meat in a pie dish, cover with the mashed potatoes, and bake in a 375 degree oven for 30 minutes. Before serving, run the dish quickly under the broiler to brown the potato crust.

Mushroom Soup from the Inn at Bree

Chop 1/2 pound of mushrooms very fine. In a large saucepan, melt 4 tablespoons of butter. Add 1 tablespoon of chopped onion, 2 cups of finely chopped carrots, 2 cups of finely chopped celery, and 1 clove of garlic, minced. Stir in 2 1/2 cups of beer broth, 3 1/2 cups of water, 1 small can of tomato paste, 1/4 teaspoon of salt, and 1/16 teaspoon of pepper. Bring to a boil. Cover and reduce heat. Simmer 1 hour. Purée the soup. Melt 2 tablespoons of butter in a skillet, add 1/2 pound of sliced mushrooms, and sauté for 5 minutes. Add to the soup. Add 1/4 cup of dry sherry. Heat thoroughly and serve.

Mirkwood Cookies

Sift together 2 1/2 cups of flour, 2 teaspoons of double acting baking powder, and 1/2 teaspoon of salt. Cream 3/4 cup of butter. Gradually add 1 cup of brown sugar (granulated brown sugar works well), creaming well. Blend in 1 unbeaten egg and 1 teaspoon of vanilla and beat well. Melt 1 1/2 squares (1 1/2 ounces) of unsweetened chocolate; set aside to cool. Add the dry ingredients gradually to the egg mixture. Mix thoroughly. Remove 2/3 of the dough to a floured pastry board. Stir 1/4 teaspoon of baking soda into the chocolate. Blend the chocolate mixture into the remaining 1/3 of the dough. Chill if necessary for easier handling. Roll half of the light-colored dough into a 10 by 4 inch rectangle. Shape half of the dark (chocolate) dough into a 10 inch roll and place on the rectangle of light dough. Mold the light dough around the dark dough and wrap in foil. Repeat with the remaining dough. Chill for at least 2 hours. Cut the dough into slices 1/8 to 1/4 inch thick. Place 2 slices together on a greased cookie sheet to resemble eyes. Pinch the corner of each slice to give a slant-eyed look to the cookie. Place a chocolate chip into the center of each eye. Bake for 8 to 12 minutes in a preheated 350 degree oven. Remove from the baking sheets at once. Store between layers of foil in a flat, covered container. Makes approximately 3 1/2 dozen cookies.

Beorn's Honey Nut Cake

Put 1 1/2 cups of cottage cheese through a strainer. Mix the strained cottage cheese with 1 1/2 tablespoons of sifted flour, 1/4 teaspoon of salt, 3 tablespoons of sour cream, 3 beaten egg yolks, 3/4 cup of honey, 1 tablespoon of butter, 1 tablespoon of lemon juice, the rind of 1 lemon, and 1/2 cup of wheat germ. Fold in 3 egg whites, stiffly beaten. Butter a 9 inch square cake pan. Sprinkle the bottom of the pan with 1/8 cup of wheat germ. Pour the batter into the pan and top with 1/8 cup of wheat germ and 1/2 cup of chopped nuts. Bake in a preheated 375 degree oven for 30 minutes.

Scotch Eggs Strider

Hard boil 8 eggs. Cool and peel. Mix together 1 pound of sausage meat, 1/2 teaspoon of sage, 1 tablespoon of parsley, and a pinch of thyme (or use 1 pound of sage-flavored sausage). With the sausage meat make 8 patties large enough to surround the 8 peeled, hard-cooked eggs. Place an egg in the center of each patty and form the sausage around the egg. Roll the egg in flour seasoned with salt and pepper, then in beaten egg, and then in bread crumbs. Fry in deep fat.

Baked Bluefish for Gollum

Preheat the oven to 425 degrees. Place a 4 to 5 pound bluefish, cleaned and split, on an oiled baking sheet, skin side down. Lay 5 or 6 strips of bacon across it. Bake uncovered for 25 minutes until the fish flakes easily. Sprinkle with fresh parsley and lemon juice and serve immediately.

Seedcake for Gimli

Preheat the oven to 350 degrees. Butter an 8-inch round cake tin. Sift 2 1/2 cups of flour with 1 teaspoon of baking powder and a pinch of salt. Cream together 4 ounces of butter and 3/4 cup of sugar. Beat 1 egg and add to the butter, then add 2 teaspoons of caraway seeds. Fold in the flour mixture, then gradually add enough milk (up to 1/2 cup) to make a smooth, thick batter. Pour into the prepared pan. Bake in the middle of the over for 45 minutes, or until a toothpick inserted in the center comes out clean. Let cool 5 to 10 minutes before turning out on a cake rack.

Goldberry's Pie

Heat the oven to 425 degrees. Mix 2/3 cup of sugar, 4 tablespoons of flour, 1/3 teaspoon of cinnamon, and a pinch of grated lemon peel. Mix with 3 cups of fresh berries (blueberries, blackberries, raspberries, strawberries, boysenberries). Pour into a pastry-lined pie pan. Dot with butter. Cover with the top crust. Brush the top crust with milk and sprinkle with sugar. Bake for 35 to 45 minutes. If the crust begins to brown too much, cover the edges with tin foil.

Roast Mutton for the Trolls

Leave a thin layer of fat on a large leg of mutton and rub with a cut clove of garlic. Roast for 25 minutes per pound in a 350 degree oven. Serve with mint jelly and Shire pudding.

Shire Pudding

Mix together 1 cup of milk, 2 eggs, 1 cup of flour, and 1 teaspoon of salt in a blender. Put 3 tablespoons of hot beef or lamb drippings in a 9 inch glass pie plate. Pour the batter into the middle of the drippings. Bake in a preheated 425 degree oven for 15 minutes. Reduce the heat to 350 degrees and continue baking until the pudding is puffy and brown.

Maps

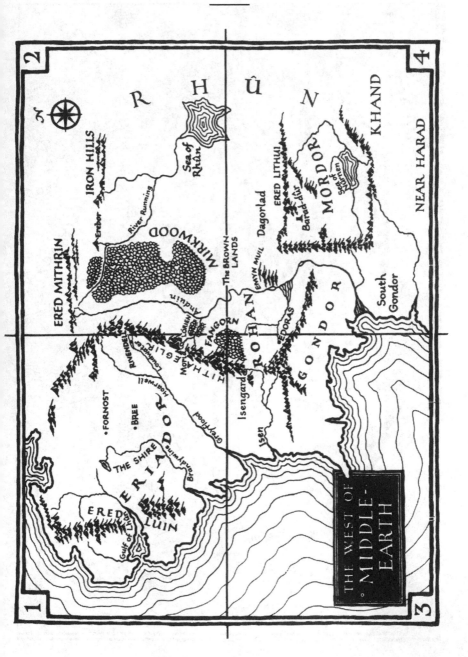

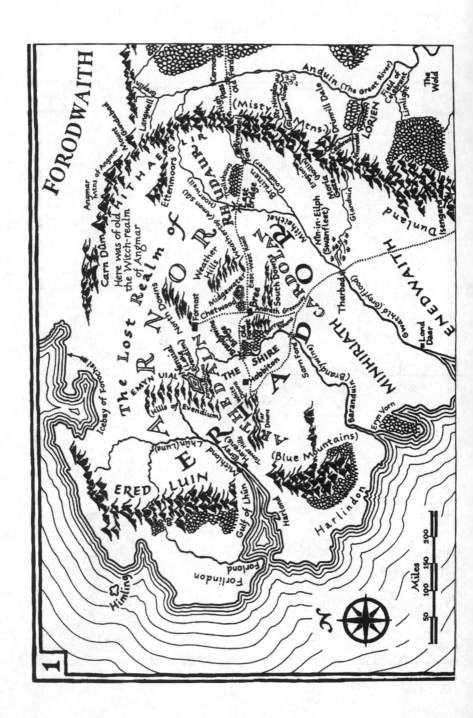

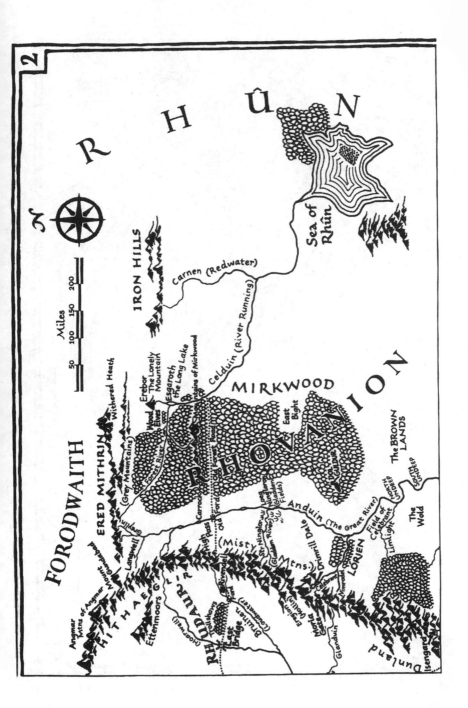

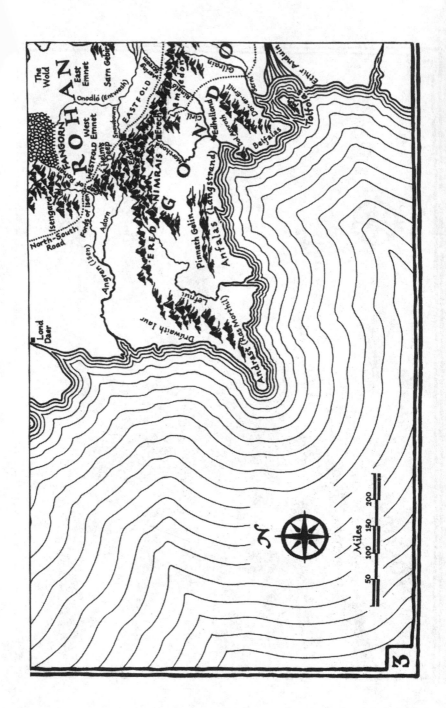

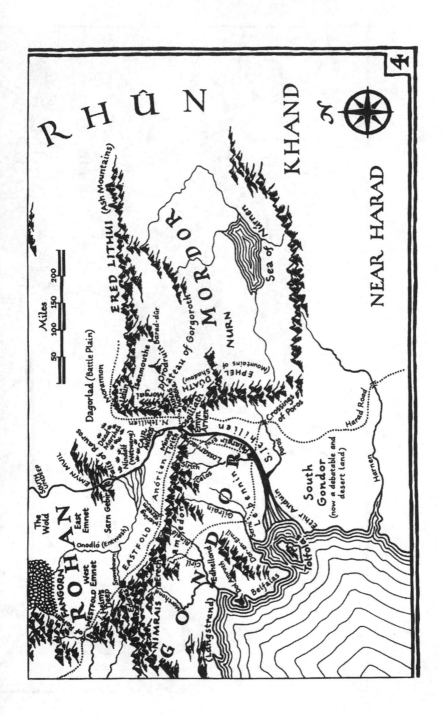

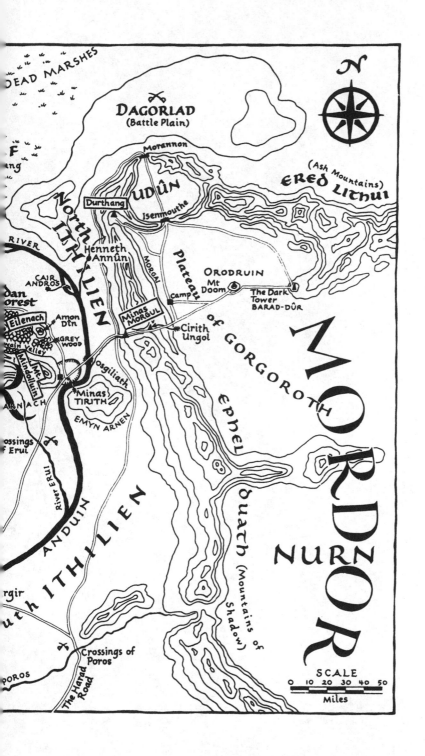

ACKNOWLEDGMENTS

"The Lord of the Rings, by J.R.R. Tolkien: Personal Best," by Scott Rosenberg. This article first appeared in Salon.com, at http://www.Salon.com. An online version remains in the Salon archives. Reprinted by permission.

"The Prevalence of Hobbits," by Philip Norman. First published in *The New York Times Magazine.* Copyright © 1967 by The New York Times Company. Reprinted by permission.

"Interview with Tom Shippey," conducted by Houghton Mifflin in May 2001. Reprinted courtesy of Houghton Mifflin Company, www.houghtonmifflinbooks.com.

"Kicking the Hobbit," by Chris Mooney. Reprinted with permission from *The American Prospect,* Volume 12, Number 10: June 4, 2001. The American Prospect, 5 Broad Street, Boston, MA 02109. All rights reserved.

"The Gods Return to Earth," by C. S. Lewis first appeared in *Time and Tide.* The review was later published as part of "Tolkien's 'The Lord of the Rings' " in *On Stories: And Other Essays on Literature,* edited by Walter Hooper, copyright © 1982 by the Trustees of the Estate of C. S. Lewis, reprinted by permission of Harcourt Brace & Company.

"Oo, Those Awful Orcs!" by Edmund Wilson. This article is reprinted from *The Nation* magazine. Copyright © The Nation Company, L.P.

"The Staring Eye," by Ursula K. Le Guin. Copyright © 1974 by Ursula K. Le Guin; first appeared in *Vector;* reprinted by permission of the author and the author's agents, the Virginia Kidd Agency, Inc.

"The Ring of Evil," from *Asimov on Science Fiction,* by Isaac Asimov. Copyright © 1981 by Nightfall, Inc. Used by permission of Doubleday, a division of Random House, Inc.

"Introduction to *J.R.R. Tolkien's Lord of the Rings (Modern Critical Interpretations),*" by Harold Bloom. Copyright © 2000 by Chelsea House Publishers. Reprinted courtesy of Chelsea House Publishers.

"Hobbits in Hollywood," by Judith Shulevitz. First published in *The New York Times Book Review.* Copyright © 2001 by The New York Times Company. Reprinted by permission.

"Does Frodo Live?" by Janet Adam Smith. First published in *The New York Review of Books.* Reprinted with permission from *The New York Review of Books.* Copyright © 1972 Nyrev, Inc.

"Lord of the Geeks," by Julian Dibbell. First published in *The Village Voice.* Reprinted by permission of the author.

Discussion questions from "A Reader's Guide to *The Lord of the Rings* by J.R.R. Tolkien." Reprinted courtesy of Houghton Mifflin Company, www.houghtonmifflinbooks.com.

"Tolkien of Affection," by Mel Rosen and "The Middle-earth Gourmet," by Maureen Bayha and Alida Becker, reprinted with permission from *A Tolkien Treasury.* Copyright © 2000, 1989, and 1978 by Running Press Book Publishers, Philadelphia and London, www.runningpress.com.